THIS BOOK THE PROPERTY
OF
JESS F. BAGLEY

THE BOOK THE PRINTERS
OF
ROBERT P. SMOOTH

Arizona the Beautiful

Hi! Marcey!

Dorothy McLaughlin

Herb McLaughlin

Don Dedera

Arizona
the Beautiful

PHOTOGRAPHS BY HERB AND DOROTHY McLAUGHLIN

TEXT BY DON DEDERA

THIS BOOK THE PROPERTY
OF
JESS F. BAGLEY

DOUBLEDAY & COMPANY, INC., GARDEN CITY, NEW YORK   1974

DEDICATION

For my parents, the newcomers
who introduced me to Arizona

Don Dedera

For the many people who have assisted us
with our photographic efforts over the years

Herb and Dorothy McLaughlin

This book is fully protected by copyright under the terms of
the International Copyright Union. Permission to use portions of this book must be obtained in writing from the
publisher.

The text of Chapter 7 appeared in the magazine *Westways,*
(August 1973) © 1973 by Don Dedera

ISBN *D-385-03336-2*
Library of Congress Catalog Card Number 73-18749
All Rights Reserved
Printed in Japan
First Edition

CONTENTS

ACKNOWLEDGMENTS

The gratitude of photographers and writer is offered to designer Joe Ascherl and editor Sally Arteseros who endured what must have seemed unending offerings of views of a state so photogenic and evocative as Arizona. Our special thanks to Harold Richardson, noted Arizona historian who previewed the text, although the writer reserves credit for what error may remain. Another distinguished Southwesterner and treasured friend, John O. Theobald, assisted with the manuscript shortly before his untimely passing, and our debt to him is acknowledged to his beloved Lillian, in double measure.

FOREWORD

To a puckish Frank Lloyd Wright it seemed that "America was tilted, and everything loose was sliding into Southern California." In a more serious mood Neil Morgan called the move to western America "the largest migration in the history of the world."

In the three decades following World War II, and its unexampled unshackling of Americans from the farms and towns of their birth, the lonely spaces beyond the Great Plains were claimed by legions of newcomers defying description in the mass. Yet young and old, penniless and wealthy, unschooled and knowledgeable, they carried common denominators. They were people broken from tradition. They were willing to take a chance. In the main they moved by choice, not accident. They tended, more so than the relatively few sons and daughters of western pioneers, to celebrate the splendors, virtues, and romance of their adopted states.

At least, it happened that way in Arizona. Chicago means "powerful" in an Indian language. So what? say Chicagoans. But a Chicagoan transplanted to Arizona was charmed to dwell in a state whose Indian name means "place where the little waters flow." The born Virginian, who would not stoop to retrieve musket balls fired in a Blue-Gray skirmish, joined an Arizona historical society to research life on the frontier. The retired glassmaker, who wouldn't drive fifty miles twice a year out of Tiffin, Ohio, bought a motor home in order to crisscross his adopted Arizona, which contains more national parks and monuments than any other state. People, who "back East" had never shown much interest in the out-of-doors, took up hobbies as lapidaries, painters, explorers, taxidermists, naturalists, observers, and anthropologists in a land where all things seemed possible for the newly freed. Newcomers shared a feeling that Arizona, in its many parts, was created especially for them.

One facet of the newcomer mystique was an enlarged (and to outsiders, overbearing) sense of pride. Arizona grapefruit just *had* to be sweeter than that of Texas. Arizona women, fairer. The sunsets, gaudier. The folks, friendlier. The country, more fulfilling of the human soul.

The passage of time, converting newcomers to old-timers, merely reinforced the belief of the immigrants that they, of their own volition, discovered a superior collaboration of warm climate, eventful landscape, outdoor challenge, enriching lore, and fascinating original peoples. If, by dark chance, a converted Arizonan was forced away for a while, he returned as did Dick Totman who lived a year in New York, learning to be a stockbroker: "I immediately drove from the airport in Phoenix to the most remote corner of Monument Valley I could find. I didn't read a newspaper or turn on a radio or talk to another human other than my wife and a few Navajo friends. I drank the air like medicine. I cleansed my mind staring at the clouds. I restored my spirit with the views. In four days I began to recover from the dehumanization of New York."

The photographers and author of this book—they from the Rockies and the Midwest and he from the East Coast—experienced every classical phase of the Arizona neophyte-turned-veteran. The windows of their homes are now crammed with rock specimens. They have waited night upon night for the bloom of a nocturnal cactus. They have retraced the route of the Butterfield Trail, and aimed imaginary rifles through the gunports of cabins of the Pleasant Valley War. Their bound and indexed copies of *Arizona Highways* are prized more highly than encyclopedia. Once, elsewhere, they were spectators; now they are participants in a chosen homeland that never disappoints them. At times, they may even offend outlanders with their incessant boasting, although that certainly is not the intent of this book!

Nor is it meant to be a detailed guide, a serious history, or a complete photographic catalogue of the forty-eighth state. Rather, this book is offered as the essence of the images and impressions awaiting the million people who elected to go seeking Arizona the beautiful, and found it waiting, in abundance.

Arizona the Beautiful

CHAPTER ONE

Space and Time

One incomparable day a modern Arizona explorer is descending Grand Canyon, and he reins in his mule at a switchback on Kaibab Trail where he can cover half a billion years of history with the palm of his hand . . .

Or perhaps he is catching his breath in a conquest of the final vertical face of the Tonto Rim, when he observes that the ledge where he clings is crusted with sea shells . . .

Or he is perching on a sand dune at sunset, to watch the shadows of thousand-foot monoliths race faster than deer across forty miles of Monument Valley . . .

Or upon a pontoon raft he is approaching the maelstrom of Lava Falls, the remnant of a flood of molten rock which eons past intercepted the rushing snowmelt of the Rockies . . .

Or he is clambering under a rancher's barbed wire fence to follow a joyful spaniel into a daisy-dappled meadow, when abruptly right beneath his nose he spies an arrowhead, exquisitely flaked, of banded gray chert from a distant quarry . . .

13

To this day Grand Canyon and its side canyons are not fully explored.

Skeleton of a great ground sloth, recovered from Pleistocene gravel deposits near Springerville, suggests a land and climate for Arizona far different from today's. Clumsy and slow, the sloth browsed lush stream beds twenty thousand years ago. Specimen is in the Geology Room of the Museum of Northern Arizona—progressive center for a broad spectrum of scientific inquiry in the Southwest.

And in those hushed moments of wonderment he may recollect the myth of the Old Ones whispered across the millenniums: How, in the beginning, *Juh-wert-a-Mah-kai,* the Earth Medicine Man, glided in emptiness, for there existed no place to stand upon; drifted in gloom, for there shone not even a spark; wandered in silence, for there vibrated nothing else within grasp of his senses. And tiring of his solitude, the Earth Medicine Man rubbed a ball of greasy soil from his breast and set the world in space. He brought forth ants to tunnel the earth and enlarge it. From ice crystals he struck the Sun and the mistress Moon, and he cast shards of a shattered diamond to light trails across the night sky. His labors attracted other deities, who participated in shaping the Earth and endowing its creatures. From the black brow of his own eye, Earth Medicine Man fashioned *Noo-ee,* the Buzzard, who with scimitar wings slashed the land into mountains and canyons so that water would gather to nurse the willow and corn and frog and quail. Then Earth Medicine Man again kneaded oily dough from his skin and molded two dolls the color of clay. They sprang to life, the first man and woman, whom Earth Medicine Man taught to love their land, on pain of punishment.

In this scrap of legend, today's Pima Indians explain the origin of themselves and of the land called Arizona. At the same time in schools young Pimas are offered a conflicting theory: that the Earth was born of gases and matured as liquids and solids, upon which for five billion years worked the forces of physics and chemistry, and that ultimately life itself evolved from a spontaneous, unsentimental marriage of molecules. The imagery and subjectivity of Earth Medicine Man, indeed!

Yet the revelations of science also are astounding: A horizontal unconformity in the planet's crust five hundred million years old. A lofty mountaintop, once a seashore. Forty-story stone towers chiseled by silicon grains and water crystals. America's Adam and Eve marching from Asia through Alaska to people the New World from Labrador to Tierra del Fuego. So it would seem from the evidence, and in Arizona, as nowhere else, primordial geology is exposed. Arizona may be in many respects the Earth's clearest window to the distant past.

And it is more than science can explain. It is brutal and thrifty beauty pleading with man to be kinder and wiser toward his natural world. No laboratory dares to analyze the witching bouquet wafted off the sunburnt Sonoran Desert after a midsummer rain shower. No apparatus exists to assay the mystical kinship of the waking pinewoods camper to the owl serenading false dawn. No scholar appears to calibrate the human courage implied in the excavations at Naco, where the spearpoints of ancient man commingle with the bones of

The cemented dome of an age-old sand dune, Rainbow Bridge, just north of the Arizona-Utah border, was carved when an entrenched meandering stream found a short cut across a horseshoe bend. The resulting bridge of salmon-pink Navajo sandstone, most easily approached from Arizona via Lake Powell, is preserved as a national monument.

Other-world shapes of Mystery Valley, a remote arm of larger Monument Valley, cast a supernatural spell over a land of optical illusions and unearthly colors. Among sculptures as tall as a thousand feet, visitors to Monument Valley Tribal Park on the Arizona-Utah border have imagined figures of temples and fortresses, witches and gods, animated dancers and busts of great men.

On the walls of dozens of prehistoric ruins tucked away in nooks of Monument Valley can be seen the handprints of long-vanished Pueblo peoples. Ancient dwellings of Arizona's Colorado Plateau are remarkably well preserved, as is Square House Ruin, shielded from the elements by its natural stone roof.

Frozen rainbows of Petrified Forest National Park were imparted by trace minerals when entire logs were buried and converted to stone one hundred eighty million years ago. Removal of petrified wood today is illegal within the park, but elsewhere in highly mineralized Arizona, gemseekers find and keep jasper, onyx, turquoise, agate, amethyst, obsidian, beryl, azurite, opal, and forty other kinds of semiprecious stones.

A blessing in the form of a disaster was genesis for the prehistoric village known today at Wupatki National Monument, near Flagstaff. In A.D. 1064 (as pinpointed by tree-ring dating of house timber), the few residents were driven away by volcanic eruptions. But fine volcanic ash spread as a moisture-saving mulch over eight hundred square miles, and farming peoples from several Arizona regions returned to cultivate bountiful fields. During the 1100s, Wupatki was home for as many as three hundred Indians whose recreation was a ball game played in a masonry court in the valley below the village.

Polychrome jars, urns, and effigy vessels found at Casa Grande ruins.

In one of many side canyons of Grand Canyon, a statistician has calculated, all of humanity could be hidden from view. If the age of earth were thought of as a day, the building of Grand Canyon would consume the final hour, and man's time on earth would be merely ten minutes. This view is from Mather Point on the South Rim.

Lotus Wrightii.

Mohave aster.

Prickly-pear cacti.

Prickly poppy bloom.

From a seldom-pictured side angle, San Xavier del Bac, near Tucson, reaffirms its title, "Most beautiful Spanish colonial mission in the United States." Founded in 1700 by Padre Kino, today it is both a delight of architecture and day-to-day sanctuary for its parish. Byzantine domes . . . a choir loft carried on vaulted arches . . . octagonal bell towers . . . Moorish fretted windows . . . Spanish flying buttresses and corbelled balconies . . . the baroque façade . . . the interior brilliant with frescoes . . . the cruciform floor plan . . . all testify to the architectural melting pot that was viceregal Mexico. Except for bells and iron from Spain, San Xavier is made of local materials, raised mainly by Pima and Papago Indians.

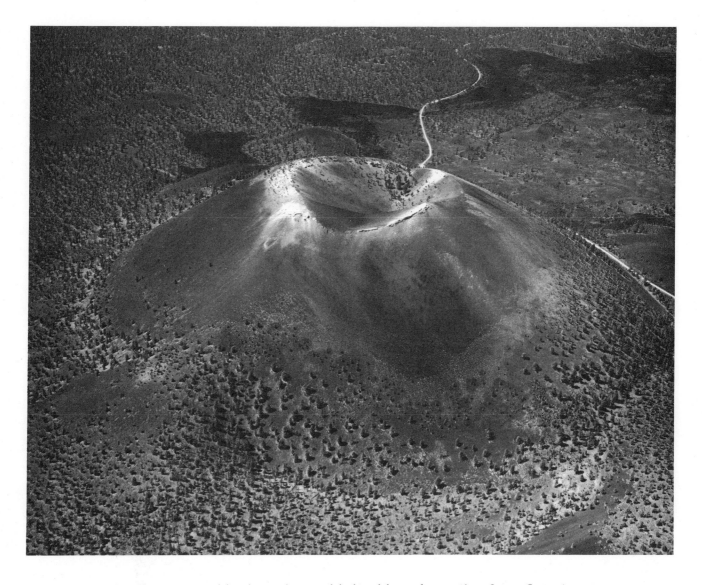

Now dormant, capped by glowing hues, and beskirted by verdant conifers, Sunset Crater in northern Arizona was violently born nine hundred years ago in earthquake, eruption, and melted rock. Boiling chemical solutions and acrid fumes finished off the symmetrical vent in sunset colors, giving a name to a national monument and the youngest feature of the San Francisco Peaks Volcanic Field. Apollo astronauts trained here for geological exploration of the moon.

An unexampled exhibit of nature's power of destruction and recovery is Meteor Crater, west of Winslow, in northern Arizona. The metallic missile that slammed into the earth was only about eighty feet in diameter, but it excavated a hole nearly three miles in circumference at the rim. At time of impact, twelve thousand years ago, all life likely was wiped out within a hundred miles. Along Meteor Crater's moonlike slopes, vehicles for lunar exploration were tested.

ponderous mammoths, long extinct. Arizona accommodates fanciful myth as well as factual theory.

Thus, without forsaking the lessons of science, it is possible to celebrate that storied place, Arizona, in allegiance with the Old Ones. To this day *Juh-wert-a-Mah-kai*'s eyebrow arches across the azure heavens, his skin-soil continues to harbor marvels of vista and life, and God's dog, Coyote, still chants cleverly around the boundaries of civilization.

Spin of earth, a day. An orbit, a year. To these, we relate. A thousand orbits. Our minds rebel, labor, falter. Now we try to conceive of a million turns around the Sun. Now *two thousand million* orbits. Impossible. It helps not at all to convert the abstraction into two billion years. Yet this is the span the Creator required to deposit and compress, elevate and lower, fracture and erode, plant and stock the Arizona of this *our* orbit.

The great geographical epochs begin with Arizona a vague, drowned trough. Through eons the trough filled with mud and sand as thick as four miles. As these deposits were transformed to stone, lava surged from deep within the Earth. More millions of years. Original rock metamorphosed to schist, gneiss, amphibolite.

Enormous upwellings of molten granite followed, accompanied by lifting of titanic mountains trending northeast. In millions of years more, tireless forces of erosion ground the mountains flat—down to their very roots—producing sediments six thousand feet thick. No sooner were Arizona's first mountains worn away, the land again heaved up into another chain of mounts, bearing northwest. And these peaks, in turn, were humbled by the ceaseless elements.

Then rolled in the tinted seas, six times overflowing deeper basins of the north and south, birthing beaches and concocting limestone of the crusty ooze of primeval life. Fierce coastal storms drove dunes to be captured intact as they hardened to colorific stone.

Again the region pulsed upward and pushed back the ocean. Silts, conglomerates, and grit were transported afar. Sand as deep as fifteen hundred feet accumulated in the north, while in the south more mountain building induced flows of melted rock and minerals.

The last sea invasions left coal in the north and limestone in the south. In the erection of the Rocky Mountains, Arizona's northern province was warped and pushed. Streams and lakes continued to carve and deposit. Slowly, ponderously, the Colorado Plateau shoved up. The central mountains diminished. Compression of monster earthquakes blocked out the southern mountain ranges. And within the remaining thirty million years, volcanic rumblings

In a sense, Tuzigoot National Monument in Arizona's Verde Valley is the remains of a sizable refugee camp of prehistory. Impoverished by an extensive drought between A.D. 1215 and 1299, Sinagua Indians abandoned their dry farms in the north in favor of the permanent, spring-fed streams from which irrigation could be drawn to water crops. By the end of the drought, ninety-two rooms clustered in Tuzigoot's small pueblo—home of a peaceful people who disposed of their adult dead in refuse piles, with little ceremony, but buried their beloved children beneath room floors, perhaps in hopes their spirits would be born again in the next children.

OPPOSITE: On a concave face of a Harquahala Mountain peak, a mountaineer applies muscle, skill, and courage. Eight Wilderness Areas are reserved in Arizona's national forest. One hundred twenty caverns have been discovered beneath the state. Although often judged from afar to be bleak and barren, Arizona in fact hosts sixty-four species of fishes, twenty-two of amphibians, ninety-four of reptiles, four hundred thirty-four of birds, and one hundred thirty-seven of mammals. Six life zones are represented: Lower Sonoran, Upper Sonoran, Transition, Canadian, Hudsonian, and Arctic-Alpine. At 114,000 square miles, Arizona ranks sixth in size among the states.

21

Nature on a madcap binge spread pads of lava, playfully etched with water, pressure, ice, sand, and wind, and gave Arizona its "Wonderland of Rocks," more formally called Chiricahua National Monument. Spires tower to one hundred seventy-six feet. Balanced rocks are stacked like children's blocks. In never-ending variety, figures of men and women and animals and things pose, cling, and rest precariously upon their pedestals covering seventeen square miles of the Chiricahua Mountains.

wracked the broken crusts. Hot basalt erupted, cooled, and hardened into dikes and necks. Around seething caldrons, cinder cones precipitated. The earth at Arizona split, folded, domed, and slid along fault lines.

And in the refinement of the final million years, the region was influenced by the cool, moist cycles of the ice ages that periodically buried the northern portions of the continent under glaciers—as recently as ten thousand years ago.

Einstein is quoted: "The real nature of things, that we shall never know—never." Within the stone pages of the grandest book of exposed geology on Earth are illustrations of early evolution. But even in Arizona the first chapters of fossilized history are missing, and we are left with a frustrating fragment: not the fossil of a worm, but the sand-filled *burrow* of a worm that slithered through ancient mud 800 million years ago. That, and a few cryptic fossils of seaweeds and algae.

With the coming of the seas, life flourished in the Age of Invertebrates: crablike trilobites and clamlike shellfish. Rudimentary sharks stalked primitive fish over coral grottos at Bisbee and Flagstaff. Experimenting with gill and lung, amphibians invented reptiles, revolutionary animals escaping imprisonment of the sea.

The beginning of the Age of Reptiles is dated at two hundred million years. As the seas retreated, swamps supported lush growth, and the uplifted land shuddered under the tread of fifty-ton dinosaurs. Pterosaurs took flight, and carnivorous phytosaurs preyed upon vegetarian giants.

In the final twenty-million-year era, warm-blooded beasts, notably mammals, dominated. Nature tested and discarded nearly two million species of birds. Through the ice ages in Arizona flourished horses as big as cow ponies, a camel as tall at the shoulder as the height of a man, a ground sloth eight feet long, at least two kinds of elephants, a rhinoceros, an antelope, a bison, a heavy-jawed wolf, and a lion weighing several hundred pounds.

To one such abundant hunting ground arrived the most formidable creatures of all—man and woman—most certainly as long ago as twelve or fifteen thousand years, as confirmed by the most significant anthropological discovery of the New World: eight stone projectile points inside the skull and rib cage of a Columbian mammoth buried in a fossil stream bed near Arizona's border with Mexico.

Possibly at first the beasts held little fear of man, and he was armed with reasoning power and history's first instrument of mass destruction, the flat, fluted, razor-sharp flint blade, securely fitted to a shaft. Early Man gorged on elephant and camel barbecue in the San Pedro Valley, and to his cave at Ventana, he carried haunches of wild horse, sloth, bison, tapir, mammoth. "A

Misnamed it may be (not a castle, and not associated with Montezuma), the cliff dwelling known as Montezuma Castle National Monument, at the geographical center of Arizona, is fitted so securely within its limestone niche, it has lasted six centuries. The original Sinagua Indian builders and occupants farmed small irrigated fields bordering Beaver Creek, and in times of danger withdrew to their fortress-apartment house of stone and mud.

thin, grim line," one Arizona scientist envisions the thousand-year southward infiltration of Asiatic peoples into the Western Hemisphere. Although the climate was benign, the people lived much like the animals they hunted. Elemental. Roving. Violent.

By 8000 B.C. the big game species were all but gone. Left with lesser herds of deer and peccary, it was man's turn to adjust or perish. The alternative was plant food: wild seeds, roots, and fruits. Around a lifestyle of gathering and cooking and storing, a higher culture, called Cochise, came into being. Cochise Man, also a nomad, lived hand to mouth, at the mercy of climate whims, yet he prevailed in Arizona, to beget two, perhaps three, even higher cultures shaped by Arizona's major geographical provinces: mountain, plateau, desert.

The mountain people were the Mogollon, drab, uninventive, borrowers of other-culture ways, but in their own right capable of basketry and potmaking, and skilled with the bow and arrow. A few centuries B.C. they acquired, likely in trade from the south, a precious sample of seeds of a food that would miraculously change their lives. When properly planted, watered, and cultivated, each fat, nutritious kernel would multiply a hundredfold. Succored by corn, the Mogollons settled down near mountain meadows, where with new-found leisure they turned artistic and stored up material wealth.

In the plateau country, where survival was less certain than in the mountains, agriculture wreaked an even more dramatic revolution among the people called Anasazi. Given corn, beans, and squash, the Anasazi congregated in interconnected apartment houses in complex pueblos. Dating from the beginning of the Christian Era, the Anasazi found stability and freedom in a certain food supply, and they responded with a flowering of arts and culture. They domesticated the dog, made music with flutes, wove baskets, perfected weapons, traded far and wide for shells, turquoise, copper bells, and parrot feathers, and worshiped in the largest rooms in prehistoric America: underground kivas seventy feet in diameter.

One of three major cliffside villages protected within Navajo National Monument, Betatakin Ruin is suggestive of a city of the future—improving its environment under an impervious dome. But Betatakin is old: A.D. 1260–77, and its vaulted ceiling counts years in the millions. The Anasazi Indians, likely precursors of modern Hopi Indians, dwelt at Betatakin.

But of all the People Who Were Here Before, the master farmers and community organizers were the Ho Ho Kam. They arrived, perhaps from Mexico, several centuries B.C., to occupy the valleys of the Salt and Gila rivers. By the year A.D. 1000 they were irrigating forty thousand acres of vegetables, fruits, and fibers from five hundred miles of precisely engineered canals. Some of their canals were seventy-five feet wide and twelve feet deep, maintaining grade across depressions through wooden flumes lined with animal hides. They delivered water on schedule to myriad farms and rationed irrigation during drought. In an achievement unprecedented in the Southwest, the Ho Ho Kam sustained a desert city six miles from the nearest water source. So successful were the Ho Ho Kam in applying their social and economic energies, they produced surplus grain and cotton for export. With relatively few tribesmen employed in food production, others had time for arts and crafts. They wove taut baskets, fashioned mosaics of turquoise, experimented in ceramics, formed cotton into cloth, carved stone vessels, and adorned their bodies with bracelets, rings, earrings, pendants. They etched sea shells with cactus acid. They cast copper bells by the lost wax method. They possibly worshiped at pyramidal temples remindful of the Aztec. Aided by Pueblo allies, they raised a watch-tower four stories above the desert floor. On a court of packed clay, two hundred feet long, they amused themselves in a game played with a rubber ball. This was the culmination of the Ho Ho Kam. Hunter became farmer. Nomad, home-maker. Savage, citizen.

And for some reason not fully understood—soil exhaustion, plague, drought—the great cultures of the Southwest were in eclipse before Columbus sailed. It is assumed that the Anasazi were predecessors of the Hopi and other pueblo tribes; that the Mogollon provided stock for several mountain tribes; that the Ho Ho Kam prevailed as the Pima and Papago, related desert tribes.

These lineal descendants of Mongolian migrants were present in Arizona to greet the soldiers of Spain, eighty years before Plymouth Rock.

26

On a desert plain near Coolidge, in south central Arizona, Casa Grande National Monument
is something of a mystery house. Archaeologists know when it was built: 1350; and that it
was raised by the Ho Ho Kam Indians, probably with the guidance of Pueblo allies. But the
purpose of Casa Grande remains uncertain. Perhaps it was a four-story sentry station, or a
fortress, or a temple, or an apartment house, or all of these. Casa Grande was abandoned by
the time Padre Kino discovered it in 1694. Today a steel umbrella wards off the worst of
destructive rains.

28

The idle doodlings of savages, of little significance? Petroglyphs—peckings on rocks—possibly as old as ten thousand years, are commonplace throughout Arizona and the Southwest. Some students have tried to infer a language from the ciphers, and other theories hold that all of the New World was thoroughly explored and mapped by the "picture rock people" thousands of years before Columbus. How else to explain a Gila River petroglyph—a complicated laby-rinth—which is an exact copy of ancient designs in Spain, Crete, and Sumatra?

29

Elephant hunter extraordinary is Dr. Emil Haury of the University of Arizona and dean of southwestern anthropologists. It was under Dr. Haury's leadership that "the most significant discovery in New World archaeology" was unearthed in southern Arizona—a kill site bearing irrefutable evidence that at least ten thousand years ago humans armed with sharply pointed stone weapons slew elephants for food. "For me," says Dr. Haury, "hunting elephants in my favorite state has been a dramatic and arresting adventure, not to be exchanged for an African safari."

As artful and ingenious as a mud-dauber's nest, the high cliff ruins of Tonto National Monument are those of a tribe called Salado, which lived along the Salt River seven hundred years ago. Long a region of intertribal trade, education, and warfare, central Arizona's mountains are covered with a mishmash of cultural relics—pit houses, delicate bird points, scrapers and knives, trade beads, grain grinders, arrow straighteners, cooking hearths. State and federal laws prohibit disturbance of antiquities.

31

Around Tubac, beginning in 1752, developed the first permanent European settlement in Arizona.

CHAPTER TWO

Where the West Began

He stands defiant, arms akimbo, his stocky torso bound by a fifty-cent alpaca coat, his calloused feet pinched into new twelve-dollar boots. He is unspeakably weary. A bullet is lodged above his right knee. Scars of other gunshot wounds mutilate his left forearm, his face, his left side, his back. A ragged saber slash brands his right leg. The top of his head is dented by a rifle butt. Now he glares at the gadfly Signal Corps photographer.

He is Geronimo, departing by train from Bowie, Arizona Territory, September 1886.

For thirty years he and his tribesmen have retarded the settlement of a land larger than France and Germany combined. Even toward the end, Geronimo with fewer than a hundred braves has tied down half the combat troops of a nation of fifty million. And now it has come to this: obscene, inquisitive camera, white man's clothing, three-thousand-mile exile, and the Fourth Cavalry Band filling his ears with brass of "Auld Lang Syne."

In the four centuries of the civilizing of Arizona are other tableaux:

Stark naked, it is said, because their garments long ago were stripped from

Still standing is the first cabin built in Prescott to house the proclaimers of Arizona Territory. In later years the chinked log structure was used as a courtroom and boardinghouse under the name Fort Misery, either for the quality of justice dispensed by Judge Howard, or the quality of food served. Actually, Fort Misery was above average for a frontier house . . . more typical is a cabin at Columbia: one room, ten by fourteen feet, unmortared log walls, one door, no windows, thatched roof, dirt floor, four gunports.

OPPOSITE: Thrusting 800 feet off the floor of Canyon de Chelly National Monument is Spider Rock. By legend a Spider Lady lives atop the spire, its tip whitened through the years by the bones of naughty Navajo children whom she has spirited away in the night.

Mortal are the mines—as this abandoned headquarters at Humboldt proves—but the lore of miners endures. On the Fourth of July, 1903, Sell Tarr, two lean yards of man, entered the jackdrilling contest at Bisbee. Tarr began at a rate of seventy blows per minute, but as soon as his drill-holder, Ed Malley, had established a true hole, Tarr stepped up the pace to eighty-five. On the changing of the thirteenth drill, Malley was stunned by a glancing blow, but he never lost his grip on the steel, and with the blood of Malley's gashed temple mixing with the drill water, Tarr drove through the granite to a new world's double-jacking record—thirty-nine and five-eighths inches in fifteen minutes, a record that has never been broken.

their bodies, three Spaniards and a Moor cross the continent to their head-quarters in Mexico. They are Álvar Núñez Cabeza de Vaca, Alonzo del Castillo Maldonado, Andres Dorantes, and the Negro slave, Estévan. Incredibly, in five years they have explored what is to become Florida, have skirted in small craft the coasts of future Alabama, Mississippi, and Louisiana, and have hiked over-land from Texas into New Mexico. And now, in 1536, only forty-three years after Columbus, the four men perhaps steal through a corner of what some day will be Arizona. From Indians they hear stories of the Seven Cities of Cíbola, far to the north.

In 1539, to a degree motivated by a lust for intoxicating drink and native maidens, Estévan reaches the Zuñi pueblos. For his excesses, he is slain. Trailing behind, Fray Marcos de Niza, the Franciscan leader, views a pueblo from a distance. In sunset the walls indeed seem wrought of gold.

Gold? In 1540 Francisco Vásquez de Coronado presses northward with crossbows, harquebuses, swords, lances, small cannon, and the first great herd of cattle to rove what will be the American Southwest.

An Italian educated in Germany, in service of Spain, Padre Eusebio Francisco Kino writes in his diary, January 1691: "Whereupon we ascended to the Valley of Guévavi, a journey of about fifteen leagues and arrived at the rancheria of San Cayetano del Tumacácori where there were some of the Sobaípuris headmen. In San Cayetano they had prepared three arbors, one in which to say mass, another in which to sleep, and a third for the kitchen." Before he is finished, Padre Kino will establish a parish of fifty thousand square miles, build twenty-four missions, found nineteen ranches, and make fifty major explorations along "the rim of Christendom."

It may not look like eight hundred million dollars today, but that's how much the mines of Jerome produced, and in its heyday the hard-working, hard-drinking hard-rock men of Jerome kept two dozen saloons humming. On terraces along a thirty-degree slope, porches overhung rooftops, and one strange day Jerome's jail broke loose and began a slow journey downhill. Today, Arizona's liveliest ghost town, Jerome is refurbished as an art colony-retirement center with an eight-hundred-million-dollar panorama of the Verde Valley.

It is 1736. Spanish prospectors find a bonanza in silver on the surface at a place called, in the Papago tongue, Arizonac, meaning "small, overflowing stream."

A mission rises near the junction of the Gila and Colorado rivers in 1781. By grandiose plan, it is to be the nucleus of a Spanish empire in North America. On July 17 the Yuma Indians annihilate the soldiers and settlers. Fray Francisco Garcéz is given one day's grace; then he, too, is executed. For the kingdom of Spain, it is the beginning of the end in Arizona.

Primed for battle against the troops of Mexico, the Mormon battalion storms into the Presidio of Tucson. The Old Pueblo is all but deserted. The volunteers run up the American flag before moving on to survey a wagon road west, in 1846.

Newsman's dispatch: "A barren, deserted, dreary waste, useful only as a dwelling place for the coyote, the owl, the rattlesnake and the prairie dog."

U. S. Senator debating Arizona Territory: "It is just like hell. All it lacks is water and good society."

In 1854 Charles D. Poston and party arrive at the banks of the Colorado after months of exploring the Gadsden Purchase. L. J. F. Jaeger's ferry rates to Fort Yuma are exhorbitant. Poston has his engineers set up their instruments and plat a townsite on the raw desert. Curious, Jaeger poles his ferry to the Arizona side. For a share in the new city, Jaeger transports the explorers to California. Eventually, from this ferry-toll survey, the city of Yuma will rise.

Early in the Civil War a strong Union force marches into Arizona from San Francisco. On April 15, 1862, scouts for the Union tangle with a small detachment of Confederates at Picacho Pass. It is Arizona's noted Civil War battle.

Memoir of John Sherman Bagg, of being age six, playing hide-and-seek in Tombstone: "I dashed to hide up Third from Fremont to Allen, past the saloon to the old OK Corral, and just as I turned, there was a shot and a man fell out of a buggy. They sent for Dr. Goodfellow. He uncovered a wound about three inches to the right of the navel. Boylike, I was as close as I could get, on my hands and knees. Dr. Goodfellow said, 'Sherman, if you are going to handle this case, I shall return to my office, but if I am to handle it, you will have to get your head out of the way.' They pulled a shutter off an office, and rolled the victim onto it, and packed him home, where he died the next day."

Thumbnail of La Paz: 1862, Pauline Weaver discovers placer gold; 1864, a bill to move the territorial capital to La Paz is defeated by one vote in the legislature; 1865, more than five thousand people are living at La Paz; 1869, the gold peters out, and the Colorado River shifts to the west; 1871, the county seat moves south to Yuma; 1873, La Paz is a ghost town.

Menu of a Prescott restaurant, 1864: "Breakfast, fried venison and chili. Dinner, roast venison and chili, or chili and beans. Supper, chili."

From the federal census, 1864, Tucson: "Peter Biaggi, clerk, Switzerland; Aloysius Maria Bosco, parish priest, Italy; John C. Clark, mechanic, New York; George Constantine, miner, Greece; Frank Cosgrove, blacksmith, Ireland; William Foster, gambler, Virginia; Alexander Geddis, teamster, Scotland; Samuel Hughes, trader, Wales; John A. James, bugler U. S. Army, Canada; Burrolo Justamente, laborer, Mexico; Ada Lovitt, housewife, Georgia; Charles H. Shibell, saloonkeeper, Missouri; Benito Soto, saddler, Mexico; George Throll, clerk, Denmark; Fernando Urquides, merchant, Spain; John Ward, glassblower, England."

Eighteen seventy-one is the year of the Camp Grant Massacre. Bands of mercenaries under white instigation fall upon a village of sleeping Apache women and children prisoners-of-war in an orgy of revenge, rape, and mutilation. President Grant exclaims, "Purely murder!" There's a trial, of course. The all-white jury is out nineteen minutes; verdict, innocent. The only surprise in Tucson is "the jury's protracted deliberation."

Phoenix is just a few years old. A soldier named Sullivan drifts through town, asking advice on the worth of some heavy black rocks he found while working on a military road. Civilian opportunists stake claims to the Silver King Mine which will yield more than six million dollars. All Sullivan gets is a job as night watchman.

The Governor's House on Pioneer Square suggests the setting for Arizona's first territorial activities, which in 1864 included the first Christmas celebration of the territorial capital. To the special delight of Prescott's seven children, a small fir was brought inside. Candles were attached with rawhide. From traveling trunks, women contributed ribbons and jewelry for ornaments. From a sack of brown sugar, a black man cooked three kinds of candy. A fiddler knew one song, "The Arkansas Traveler." The girls received gifts of rag dolls sewn by their mothers; the boys got soldiers and boats whittled by their fathers.

42

Still in private ownership and used as a residence is this taut cabin of squared timbers and hand-quarried stones on the main street of the town of Pine. Founded by Mormon pioneers from Salt Lake City in the 1870s, Pine has hung on, through good times and bad, along Pine Creek under the Mogollon Rim. Dwindling old-timers recall that by 1890 a million and a half head of cattle ranged the territory . . . and that by 1895 a quarter of a million head perished in drought.

43

In the autumn of 1871, three hundred Apaches are camped on Iron Mountain. Pima scouts overwhelm them and capture a six-year-old boy, Wassaja. He is sold to a white man for thirty dollars in silver. Renamed Carlos Montezuma, he graduates with honors from the University of Illinois medical college and goes on to distinguish himself nationally as physician and social critic.

By demand of white women, a pants tree is designated on the outskirts of Phoenix. Indian men heading into town must don a pair of pants at the tree. On departure, they rehang the pants on the tree.

"Here lie the Harris family killed by Apaches 1873"—in Hunt Canyon, a grave marker carved by a soldier from a whiskey cask. This is the year the Prescott *Miner* publishes a list of four hundred persons killed by Indians.

"WANTED—A nice, plump, healthy, good-natured, good-looking, domestic and affectionate lady to correspond with. Object, matrimony. Such a lady can find a correspondent by addressing the editor of this paper. If anybody doesn't like our way of going about this interesting business . . . it's none of their business."—The Yuma *Sentinel,* 1875.

Writes George Parsons in his diary after an 1879 worship in a church with a canvas roof in Tombstone: "Dance hall racket in rear. Calls to rally to the Lord do not mingle well with 'Hug your gals in the corner.'"

A letter is mailed from Camp Grant, April 2, 1879, to Contract Surgeon D. M. McPherson at Camp Apache, eighty-five straight-line miles distant. Thirty-nine days later Dr. McPherson receives the letter.

Ad in the *Weekly Arizona Miner,* 1882: "James Stewart's Stage Line. Carrying U. S. Mails and Wells, Fargo & Company's Express, Prescott to Gillett, Phoenix, Maricopa, etc. daily. Prescott to Skull & Peeples Valleys, Antelope, Wickenburg, Vulture, and Phoenix tri-weekly. Time to Phoenix, 24 hours."

An Estey organ is shipped around the horn and freighted to Casa Grande. It is strapped upon the back of a gigantic mule, which is driven from Picket Post twenty miles into the Pinal Mountains. To keep the organ balanced on the mule, men walk with poles along either side of the trail. The organ arrives undamaged at Pinal Ranch, there to join other treasures of eastern import: an 1850 Florence sewing machine, Ironstone and Wedgwood china, autographed first editions.

Elliott's *History of Arizona Territory* of 1884 reports that there are 75,000 settlers, running 700,000 head of cattle, and digging up eight million dollars worth of metal. There are sixty-five churches and thirty-three newspapers and only a hundred and six felons in Yuma prison. The governor is paid $216.66 per month, and it is the boast of the sheriff of Phoenix that he had to arrest only two citizens in his first four months of office.

David Declay, age eighteen, enlists as an Indian scout, number G-13, to pursue unconquered Apaches. He will stay in the army until 1929, take honorable retirement, and die in 1957 at East Fork, "the last of the Indian scouts."

Of June 1886, army wife Martha Summerhayes writes, "I had been at Tucson before, but the place seemed unfamiliar. I looked for the old tavern; I saw only the railroad restaurant. We went in to take breakfast before driving out to the post of Fort Lowell, seven miles away. Everything was changed. Iced cantaloupe was served by a spic-and-span waiter; then, quail on toast. 'Ice in Arizona?' It was like a dream, and I remarked to Jack, 'This isn't the Arizona we knew in '74.'"

Pompous General Miles hits upon a scheme to offset the Apaches' freedom of movement. A heliograph system is installed that can move a twenty-five-word message four hundred miles in two hours.

For Duett Ellison, the boys next door are the gunfighters of the Pleasant Valley War. She collects their autographs in a book with a flowery cover. "Sincerely your friend, Glenn Reynolds, Aug. 16, 1888," is an inscription, and next year Sheriff Reynolds will be slain by the Apache Kid. "Miss Duett," reads another, "may your life be long and happy is the wish of your friend, C. H. Blevins, June 30, 1887." Forty-one days later eighteen-year-old Hamp Blevins will be shot out of his saddle in the first open skirmish of the war. "In a chain of friendship pray regard me as a link, Will C. Colcord." Colcord will survive as the feud's last man. And Miss Duett? She will be the wife of the first state governor of Arizona.

Frontier Winslow has one oasis of civilization, the Harvey House railroad inn with a menu of delicacies and pretty waitresses. The temptation is too much for a roundup crew one day in 1890. The cowboys roar into town, grimy, bewhiskered, aromatic, and dressed like bums. The horrified manager intercepts them at the door of the main dining room. "Coats are required," he says. Whereupon the ramrod of the outfit leads his men back to their horses. The cowboys don their boot-length, fish-oil raincoats. Back at the dining room the foreman tells the manager, "Now, sir, we are wearing our coats!" The manager negotiates: he will feed the men free, in the kitchen. "Agreed," says the cowboy boss Henry Fountain Ashurst, who two decades later will be one of Arizona's first congressmen.

Of Wyatt Earp, the *Works* of Hubert Howe Bancroft states: "To him, more than any other man, is due the credit for driving out the banditti of the Territory. He is tall, slim, of florid complexion, blue eyes, large nose, and quick as a cat. Socially, he would be taken for a Minister."

Somewhere, it is said, the Nineties are gay. But gaiety is an emotion afforded

Eighty years of weathering and vandalism diminished Mission San Jose de Tumacácori before it came under the jurisdiction of the U. S. Park Service as a national monument. Now maintained in its ruined state, Tumacácori little resembles the elaborate sanctuary-fortress conceived by Franciscan fathers and built by Indian workers in two decades of the early nineteenth century.

by few in the southern valleys of Arizona in the last decade of the nineteenth century. Life is a trickle of water diverted by a fragile brush dam. Life is a mortgage at 18 per cent. Life is sunup labor and sundown chores. In 1890 there are 25,000 residents in Maricopa County. "All," an editor wryly observes, "living in ease, comfort, and even luxury." That may be credible to eastern investors, but not to the folks whose highways are mud, whose floors are earth, whose crops and markets are capricious, and whose children are preyed upon by faceless plagues. The Salt River is savior and scourge. One day it recedes out of reach of parched fields. Next day, the river pours into the doorways of the city. Not until 1911 with Roosevelt Dam will the river be tamed in America's first reclamation project. The Gay Nineties will arrive twenty years late in Arizona.

February 1894. Territorial Governor Nathan O. Murphy spends the night stranded in the middle of the Salt River crossing at Tempe when his stagecoach breaks a wheel. One train per day connects Phoenix to the main line at Maricopa. Shoes are two dollars a pair, twenty-five pounds of pink beans a dollar, and six bars of Bull Soap twenty-five cents. The Valley Bank of Phoenix attains a capitalization of $100,000. For two bits, Quong Hing, across from City Hall, will serve a sumptuous turkey dinner. At the Phoenix Opera House, Daniel Sully appears in *The Millionaire*. The sensation of the month: "A small boy got into the engine house last evening and sounded the fire alarm."

According to the 1895 Phoenix city directory: "The present volume contains 2,116 names (not including Chinese and many other objectionable classes), being a gain over the last publication of 361." Peter Blinn, cigarmaker. P. H. Coyle, freighter. Joseph Coulson, harnessmaker. J. H. Estarbrook, capitalist. Thomas Hickey, wagonmaker. John Gregg, carriage painter. E. E. Ford, assayer.

"Alf DeVore heard in Globe that Mama had newmonia. He forked his pony and headed for his ranch—sixty-mile ride that day. Changed horses and lit out for Medicine Camp, as a cowboy had told him he's seen Dad and me thar.

Rows of barred, sun-baked cells housed some three thousand convicts during a thirty-three-year span of Arizona's territorial years. Within the state park at Yuma today remain a block of dungeons carved from a rocky hill, a main guard tower armed with a Gatling gun, and the wry inscriptions of prisoners adorning cell walls. Most famous inmate was Pearl Hart, female armed robber, who based a successful stage career on her stories of "the hell hole" at Yuma.

48

He covered the fifteen mile by midnight but found we was gone, so followed the trail to Pole Corral. We'd left thar. He lit matches to find our sign. When he got to our camp we was out on the trapline . . . so he left me a note. It was thirty miles back to his ranch. He'd rode a hundred twenty mile horseback in thirty hours without rest."—Memoir of Cibecue Slim Ellison in *Cowboys Under the Mogollon Rim.*

From a Texas newspaper: "ANOTHER CHEAP STATE. It is astounding to find the admission of the Territory of Arizona as a state reported favorable by the Senate Committee on Territories. . . . Arizona at the last census had a population of 59,620; of these less than 24,000 were males of voting age. There were more people in the city of Fall River . . . than in all the Territory of Arizona. Nearly ten such states could be populated by the city of Boston alone. To give such a handful of people three votes in the electoral college, two seats in the Senate, and one in the House, is an absurdity."

The Phoenix *Enterprise* in 1900: "A wide open town is Phoenix at present. Gambling halls are cheered by girls and liquor is sold in the same room, thus embracing three great evils under one big tent. It is not difficult to answer the question, 'Where is your boy tonight?'"

Statehood. Grandma Champie at her ranch near Castle Hot Springs begins accepting pay from the tourists who stop at her porch asking for food and bed. Word of the place spreads. Well-to-do guests build their own cottages around the central house. As far as Grandma could ever learn, Champie Ranch becomes Arizona's first ranch operated mostly for dudes, who will draw recreation from ways of life that had been so desperate for so long, on the frontier.

Bawling and shuffling, Hereford cattle are rounded up on a desert range north of Phoenix.

CHAPTER THREE

The Desert

By unlikely legend the surveyors of Arizona lands, newly purchased from Mexico in 1854, were heading due west toward the Gulf of California, when a few miles beyond Nogales they thirsted for a drink, ran the international boundary northward toward Yuma, and thereby deprived Arizona of a seacoast. Thus, until California breaks off and sinks, the desert must double as ocean for landlocked Arizona.

The notion has merit. Desert is also skyscape and salt crust, tempest and repose, tangy air and trackless space. Between remote ports and mountain islands bounds a main of dust and alkali. And here and there dwell dehydrated castaways, marooned by sealike mirages.

If this arid province truly were a body of water, it would equal the combined size of the three largest Great Lakes—and provide an arcing passage comparable to that lying between New England and the Carolinas. The high and low deserts, which dominate the west and south, comprise nearly two-thirds of Arizona and extend from the leached fjords of Lake Mead through the dune beaches of Yuma across the rolling earth swells of the border counties into the

51

southeastern corner, so much resembling an elevated archipelago. This realm is as formidable and compelling as any in America; worthy, this arid ocean, of an exploratory voyage.

As precautionary as sailors, we provision at Kingman, seat of Mohave County, which surprisingly boasts a thousand miles of bona fide shoreline along the Colorado River and its lakes. But inland, it is a country "where you dig for wood and climb for water," a land of crests dotted with dripping springs, and troughs burying parched skeletons of trees. We take aboard water, knowing that on the Arizona desert humans may lose as much as a quart of liquid per hour. In a pinch we could fill out a menu of dove eggs, smoked squirrel, boiled yucca buds, mesquite-bean soup, salad of tomatillo and miner's lettuce and wild onion, spit-roasted quail, fried cactus root, baked mescal hearts, prickly pear fruit, and Mormon tea. Our pampered stomachs would rather not—so canned and packaged rations are stowed aft, along with a man-size shovel, a tow chain, a large signal mirror, matches, and a first-aid kit.

Then, on a spanking breeze, we run and beat down Mohave, fifth largest county in the nation. Swells race through precise stands of creosote bush at bone-dry Red Lake. Aquamarine groves undulate toward the Cottonwood Cliffs. Dust devils like desiccated waterspouts spin down the bed of the Big Sandy River. When hounded by squalls, we bend under the lee of an island-in-the-sky, the Hualapai Range rearing a mile above the surrounding plain, and dash into the sanctuary of the ghost town of Oatman.

The inhabitants are deserving of a Gulliver. A race called Black Mountain Pensioners, they number only two hundred—all that remain from the boom between the great world wars, when Oatman's population swelled to twenty thousand, with two banks, seven hotels and twenty saloons. Stubborn and resourceful, the Pensioners spruce up board-and-batten hillside homes, make do with retirement checks, and cling to the mystique of an earlier, golden day. ("You're looking at three million dollars, mister, right there in those tailings dumps.") They keep mineral claims active, against the time when the price of gold once again will overtake labor costs. They patronize the Brown Jug Saloon and the Gold City Hotel, fifteen rooms beginning at five dollars, bathrooms down the hall, which was good enough for the honeymoon of Clark Gable and Carole Lombard in 1939. The Pensioners hold Sunday swap meets at the foot of Main Street. Friday nights the hotel feeds suppers reminiscent of the board-inghouse fare once set before the steel-muscled men who wrenched the ore from the earth. The Pensioners maintain an antique sheriff's office, allow burros to wander the streets, and treat aliens with faultless courtesy unless a critical word is said about gold. We note a scrawl on a weathered wall—"Free enter-

Adorning an otherwise spindly and unimpressive night-blooming cereus is a saucer-sized star of multiple points and fragrance that carries a quarter of a mile. In a single night of glory the bloom opens, attracts birds to help in pollination, and closes before dawn, never to open again. A water-storing bulb beneath the cactus may weigh as much as a hundred pounds.

Patterns of nature and man meld near Yuma, where irrigation from the Colorado River and wells transforms desert to productive farmland.

Under these repelling bluffs, President Theodore Roosevelt, in 1911, stepped down from his open touring car, slapped his duster, lifted his goggles, and proclaimed, "The Apache Trail combines the grandeur of the Alps, the glory of the Rockies, and the magnificence of the Grand Canyon, and then adds an undefinable something. . . . To me it is the most awe-inspiring and most sublimely beautiful panorama nature has ever created."

54

prise! Gold miner! Don't tread on me!" We respect local custom and revel in hospitality before returning down old U. S. 66—once "The Main Street of America" and Steinbeck's "Glory Road"—where it streaks straight out into the desert.

The sun is the undisputed god of life's *immense enduring* in the land of much heat and little water. The sun gives all, takes all. As nowhere more ingeniously, life specializes for efficiency.

Consider: of 3,370 species of plant life catalogued in Arizona, some 1,500 are descendants of a rose that through two hundred centuries shed its leaves to reduce transpiration, thickened its stem to store water, and organized its spines to repel animal invaders. Cacti, most diversified of the drought-resisters, are the fifty-foot-tall saguaro and the thumbnail-size pincushion, each surviving extremes of radiation and drought. A cactus may be shaped by flat pads (the prickly pear), or be covered by thousands of spines (the cholla), or be outfitted with an expandable accordion skin (the barrel), but the object is the same: acquire and husband water.

The giant saguaro may drink a ton of water from a single rain, through hairy lateral roots only a few inches below the surface of the desert floor. But cacti are not the only ingenious adaptations on the desert. The pea family occurs as trees of small and tentative leaf. The ghostly smoke tree, seldom in foliage, insures propagation with hard-shelled seeds which must be scratched by flood action before sprouting. The slow-growing ironwood forms wood so dense it will shrug off a woodsman's ax. The paloverde manufactures food in its green bark. The mesquite sinks roots as long as two hundred feet and drops nutritious beans whose germination is enhanced by digestion of animals.

Some lilies have gone underground, storing moisture in fibrous bulbs. Other lilies, the yuccas, through evolution have struck unique, mutually beneficial agreements with moths. A moth at one plant rolls up a ball of pollen, flutters to the flower of another plant, deposits its eggs in the ovules. Then, with no reward of nectar—the moth seems capable of inductive thought—it climbs the flower's stigma and tucks the ball of pollen inside to fertilize the flower. In time the flower produces a pod around the moth eggs. Grubs hatch when seeds ripen. They eat relatively few seeds, bore out of the pod, and sleep in the ground until spring. To compound the astonishment, each species of yucca is in partnership with its own kind of moth.

Annuals are drought-evaders, risking perpetuation of species in seeds which lie dormant through dryness, stir alive in warm wetness, and hurry to completion of another generation of seeds. During infrequent years when pacific storms soak the southwestern basins, Arizona deserts burst alive to rival the phytoplankton of the Arctic Ocean in summer. Milkweeds, pin-flowers, blue dicks, buckwheats, four-o'clocks, and mustards smear the flats in riotous color. Entire slopes are enriched by golden poppies, and travel lanes are lined by blue lupine and peach mallow. And if the promise of a moist spring proves premature, seeds of desert annuals know how to wait. Only half will germinate in ideal conditions. Thereafter, only half of the remaining half, so that always some seeds will exist to conquer prolonged drought.

Animals of the desert mostly are evaders of dryness and heat, although some have devised marvelous means of coping. The desert tortoise magically appears (old-timers swear) when and where it will rain, and drinks a pint of water to last a season. The antelope ground squirrel owes its existence not so much to succulent forage, as to a highly efficient kidney. More amazing is the kangaroo rat which satisfies its water need by breaking down the carbohydrates of dry seeds, never taking a drink of free water from birth to death. Tenacity personified is the spadefoot toad which waits underground in lowlands for rain to form a temporary pond. Only then does the toad emerge to breed. One month after conception, functioning adults take on enough water to last most of a year and burrow into the earth for a long sleep.

For those animals which are active through all seasons, night is favored for feeding and traveling. And when we see them, it is usually at dusk or dawn. They, too, are distinctive of form and habit. The desert bighorn sheep can climb sheer cliffs, go five days without water, and detect the wave of a man's hand a mile away. The collared peccary, in herds of eight to twenty, attack cacti hoglike through the roots (and even straight on). Of lizards, well known is the chuckawalla which, when threatened, will dart down a fissure and inflate its body with air.

Birds, too, have accommodated to the desert, tempted by cactus fruit and seeds, periodic swarms of insects, and other animals upon which to prey. With their mobility, many birds may migrate to kinder climates, but those that stay must fill a niche. The Gila woodpecker and gilded flicker excavate water-cooled apartment houses in giant cacti. The cactus wren hides its nest amid the cruelest of cholla. By teamwork, Gambel's quails decoy the poisonous, egg-lusting Gila monster. The Sonoran white-rump shrike, lacking the talons of the hawks, impales its victims on a thorn for butchering. In winter, the desert poorwill goes into a torpor, its breath and heartbeat all but stopped. An amusing cuckoo is the road runner, but not to the rattlesnake providing its breakfast. One twilight of our desert cruise we tie up at a water hole to study loose flocks of evening grosbeak, a pair of raspberry linnets in full song, feisty white-

At home between barrel and giant cactus, a flock of mourning doves makes a roost of blooming ocotillo.

Hedgehog cacti.

Fairy duster.

Apache Lake along the Apache Trail.

Superstitions and snow.

Cholla cactus, Arizona desert in April.

Owl's clover carpet, Apache Trail.

Storm and dunes.

Unpaved track, Bill Williams Mountain.

A summer soaking for Mohave.

The rolling grasslands near Elgin, north of the Huachuca Mountains, have only partially recovered from overgrazing by pioneers' herds. One victim is the masked bobwhite quail, plentiful in southern Arizona before the turn of the century.

Rising steeply more than a thousand feet, Vermilion Cliffs rim the eastern side of Houserock Valley.

crowned sparrows bullying meeker souls, and ranks of mournful Inca doves. Overhead a prairie falcon has no need of binoculars as it scans the shadows for the slight movement of fur that will precipitate another violent act in the desert's savage cycles.

For a day in the sun we choose the Apache Trail, Arizona's favorite Sunday drive and the most democratic road in all of motordom. Presidents and kings have braved the tilted grades and tight curves through the Superstition Range east of Phoenix, and come back humbler beings. The ups and downs of the Apache Trail likewise have had a leveling influence on treasure hunters, dustbowl immigrants, renowned scientists, movie actresses, salon photographers, and civil servants. They, along with legions of campers, boatmen, hikers, and picnickers, have melded an Apache Trail brotherhood.

The common denominator is the chance to do and feel as much, or little, as one wants. Around Superstition Isle the perimeter loop passes conifer and cactus, lake and peak, adventure and retreat. To each his memories: bucked off a mare into a prickly pear patch; caught in the smoke of a runaway brushfire; warned away by a gunshot from a paranoid gold prospector. And quieter reflections: drifting lazily after bass on a balmy afternoon; lying in a sleeping bag under heavens so transparent a satellite could be seen tumbling between the stars.

Once-rustic Apache Junction, portal on U. S. Highway 60, has matured as a cozy base for Apache Trail journeys. Here are resorts and supermarkets and headquarters for packers who guide expeditions into the Superstition Wilderness. We pause for checking of tires and radiator. Also flourishing at Apache Junction are a dozen retail outlets for Lost Dutchman Gold Mine maps. We purchase one, despite thickening suspicion that, really, if somebody had the way to the bonanza, he wouldn't sell it for fifty cents.

We Arizonans know to circle the Superstitions clockwise, outbound via State Highway 88, with return by U. S. 60. That way, on most of the hairpin turns, our car hugs the cliff while approaching traffic is obliged to skirt the scary outer edge. The road's safety record is surprisingly good, but even for old hands, serenity is the inner lane. And so, we begin, allowing at least eight hours for the hundred thirty-five miles. The scenery starts a step out of town. Western ramparts of the Superstitions rear in ragged disorder behind a sweep of Sonoran scape. Saguaros lift imploring limbs to cumulous clouds; paloverde and ironwood don smocks of lemon and lavender. Ocotillo brandish fiery torches. Agave sacrifices in gaudy reproduction. Yucca in regal ermine affirms rebirth.

Great horned owl

Kit fox

Desert tortoise

Gila monster

Collared peccary (javelina or wild pig)

59

Road runner, or chaparral cock, once restricted to the American Southwest, is said to be extending its range through Arkansas eastward, and northward along the West Coast.

We pause at the Bluebird Mine, an authentic gold dig opened by the owners for public inspection at a fee, then follow the tortuous track through rolling chaparral to Tortilla Flat. Named for pancakelike rock formations, the wide spot harbors a back-country grocery, bait shop, and refreshment stand. And, alas! more maps to the lost mine. We show the owners our own Lost Dutchman map, and satisfied that we have paid our way, they describe road conditions ahead. The pavement ends five miles past Tortilla Flat, and the Apache Trail thereafter is unsurfaced but well maintained for twenty-four miles to Roosevelt Lake. Barring flash floods, this portion of the trail is the reason for going. So spectacularly Burmese, it was chosen as location for the movie, *The Burma Road.*

60

Wax-white bloom of giant saguaro is the official state flower of Arizona, and harbinger of figlike fruit and seeds which Indian women ground into a nutritious flour. For mile upon mile, in May and June, saguaros bear bouquets in their arms and wear tiaras on their heads.

Descent of Fish Creek Hill is fifteen hundred feet in a mile and a half, around a box canyon. Undercut, lichen-stained Walls of Bronze loom over a creek bed of sycamores, cottonwoods, and willows, a likely place to jump a deer. This day it is a javelina, comically bounding on stubby legs through yucca stalks. The trail passes geology named by cattlemen and freighters: Old Woman's Shoe, Eagle Rock, Flat Iron Mountain, Dying Warrior, the Pyramids. Down Fish Creek Hill we meet a Kansas farmer who drives the inner lane *in both directions.* In the middle of a switchback his knuckles are white on the wheel and his eyes are fixed on his hood; his wife seems to be lecturing, "Now, Hiram, there's no guard rail here." We old salts trade rights-of-way, and our tires pitch

61

stones down a hundred-foot drop. No snobbery is more superior to that of the veteran of Fish Creek Hill!

Then, at a lake, we swim. Watch water-skiing. Broil a steak over mesquite coals. In siesta, decide to pause at Roosevelt Dam. Now surpassed by monumental concrete dams, Roosevelt retains its distinction of the world's tallest masonry dam, at two hundred eighty-four feet. An hour of prowling its innards sharpens respect for the government engineers, Italian stonecutters, and Apache laborers who conceived and executed the nation's first major reclamation project. Everything for the dam, save stone, was brought along the Apache Trail. Tour completed, we review the options: a stop at the old damsite village, or a visit to an Indian ruin national monument, or backtrack to view the trail's mirror vistas, the outside lane of Fish Creek Hill be damned. But we elect to press on around the circle, toward the copper towns of Globe and Miami. Along the way the parapets retreat, allowing the canyons to hold a patch of ground here and there, enough for a pasture or a corral. By the time the Apache Trail rejoins U. S. 60 at Cobre Valley, the land is so tame it grows a golf course.

"Beware, lest you, too, succumb to the lure of the Lost Dutchman Mine."

The official state highway department road sign beneath the stern, alien face of the Superstition Range can scarcely be ignored. Yet it has gone unheeded by a wonder-struck procession.

Jacob Walz, himself, must have relished his shadowy role. He lent substance to tall tales of Spanish gold when he appeared in Phoenix with his pockets allegedly bulging with rich ore. Attempts to follow him invariably failed, and it's said that more than a few trackers of the Dutchman were never heard from again.

Whether Walz reopened a Spanish lode or stole choice ore from a contemporary mine elsewhere, before his death in 1891 he gave a box of gold nuggets to a friend in Phoenix. The Dutchman's own map misled those who tried to follow it. Into the twentieth century, the trek into the Superstitions has been fueled by admirable perseverance, gullible enthusiasm, and sensational violence. The quest has claimed some fifty victims in recent years, most of them to exposure and exhaustion.

Adolph Ruth was perhaps the first of the "modern" blunderers. He went alone into the Superstitions in 1931. Years later his headless torso was found, and some distance away, his skull, pierced by a bullet. In similar fashion in 1948 one James Cravey was dispatched.

As a hobby, methodical, scholarly Sims Ely pursued the Dutchman like a private detective. He assembled a fast-reading book, but no pot of gold.

The tawny band rimming the western face of the Superstition Mountains (by Pima belief) was the foam of the Great Flood. And those grotesque granite figures engulfed by the spume are the cowardly unfaithful, turned to stone by their angry god. From such legends, the Superstitions take their name.

63

Bajadas, the Mexicans call them, the great alluvial slopes of the Sonoran Desert—and nowhere are they more fascinating than in Organ Pipe Cactus National Monument, some five hundred square miles along the international border in southwestern Arizona. Besides the multiarmed organ pipes, the park protects thirty other species of cacti. At Quitobaquito Springs, more than a hundred fifty species of birds have been sighted.

Among others: Al Morrow, a quarter century of solitary searching, in his spare time, in laborious longhand, translated the Bible into the vernacular. Celeste Marie Jones, former opera star, bossed mountaintop excavations that cost several lives. Ed Piper, weathered ascetic, who with one hand planted peach trees and rose bushes and with the other fatally shot a rival. Piper later died with his boots off, in a hospital, of ulcers.

And more. The Englishman who announced discovery simply by reading books in London. The Arizonan who spent $3,000 for aerial photography. The California woman who claimed as an Indian captive to have been shown the gold bars stacked like cordwood in a cavern. Bill Hughes who, in 1962, announced he had found the mine and, by way of proof, washed out a show of color in the drinking fountain of the newsroom of the state's largest newspaper. A furrier in Alsace, read of the mine, sold everything and traveled 8,000 miles to search futilely for six years. In recent times, Harry Van Suitt staked claims to 10,000 acres. And every year, more thousands go with the Dons Club to retrace the Dutchman's footsteps.

One man extracted from the Superstitions a treasure more precious than gold. Retired from the Navy, Dewey Wildoner went for twenty-five years as hiker, explorer, and photographer into the wilderness, returning each time with health, knowledge, and peace of mind. "It is a living picture of the country as seen by pioneers," says he. "An opportunity for spiritual enrichment."

As for material reward, Oren Arnold likely holds the record. He candidly admits that two hours of writing a brief booklet returned $14,000 in royalties. Says he:

"So far as I can learn, I am the only person who has acquired any treasure from the mine since the Dutchman himself died."

In the thirty years following the Gold Rush of 1849, hundreds of treasure seekers lost their lives along Camino del Diablo, the Devil's Highway, hugging the international border for a hundred and fifty miles east of Yuma. To this day a raw reserve of Arizona-Mexico desert is without a single permanent human inhabitant. But these unpeopled fastnesses are now the exception, as technology and transportation make life plausible where once it was impossible. Today the relatively uninhabited spaces of southern Arizona are the islands-in-the-sky, withdrawn as game refuges and national monuments and forests.

We consult our charts. Our steering wheel becomes a dial for change of climate. In terms of life zones, the short drive from Tucson to the top of the Santa Catalina mountains equals a fifteen-hundred-mile journey to Canada—from ten inches of precipitation per year to thirty, from swimming pools to ski slopes, from tumbleweed to fir, from shirt sleeves to mackinaw. Much the same holds true of the Santa Ritas, the Quinlins, the Baboquivaris, the Bradshaws, the Whetstones, the Dragoons, the Pinals, the Galiuros, the Santa Teresas.

Two hundred species of birds comprise a life list in Madera Canyon, and in the Coronado National Memorial on the south shoulders of the Huachuca Mountains, visitors sight wildlife of the semitropics: coati-mundi, ocelot, jaguar, thick-billed parrot.

Where to go this day? Miller Peak, towering over Fort Huachuca, an incongruous combination of space-age-electronics laboratories and moldering horse-cavalry quarters? Mount Graham, at 10,713 feet, bearing a magnificent stand of Englemann's spruce and guarding nineteen packloads of gold buried by Mexican bandits? Cochise Stronghold, where the greatest Apache chief rests in a secret grave?

Not this day. We choose the Chiricahuas, with five climatic zones to 9,795 feet, in the extreme southeastern corner of Arizona. As we climb, desert heat falls behind, one degree for every three hundred feet of elevation. At Chiricahua National Monument we hike where precocious nature doodled. Lava pads spread a million years ago are etched by water, pressure, ice, sand, silt, and wind. There are spires and balanced rocks—one weighs six hundred tons and rests on a three-inch base. "We've been accused," says the ranger on duty, "of hiring a full-time sorceress to maintain the whammies on our balanced rocks."

The concept of a cool, moist sky-island set off by contradicting expanses is exemplified by the Chiricahuas. Forty miles long and twenty wide, the range lifts twin peaks to nearly 10,000 feet elevation, off the semidesert plains of the San Simon and Sulphur Springs valleys. Here, man, animal, and plant are granted asylum. Apaches and outlaws once rested and resupplied here, and now their camps serve the family of a smelter worker from nearby Douglas, and the world's foremost spider scientist from faraway New York. Fat beeves graze ranges fenced by pioneer cowmen. White-tailed deer pilfer apples planted by women of the frontier. Occasionally a lobo wolf will navigate from a Mexican sky-island northward to the Chiricahuas, and remind moderns of last century's perils. But as we crisscross the Chiricahuan trails, all is peace. Where Curley Bill Brocius bullied the entire town of Gayleyville, wild turkeys scratch among the ruins. Within the Apache redoubt, Cave Creek Canyon, carpeted and draped with grass and trees and walled in by lichen-stained turrets and walls, a bird-watching couple from Santa Monica stalk the coppery-tailed trogon with a 500-millimeter lens. Before the sagging false fronts of wicked old Paradise, a high school art class brushes oil on canvas.

On a sacred mountain in the heart of an ancient Indian homeland sprawls Kitt Peak National Observatory, housing one of man's modern miracles—the Robert R. McMath Solar Telescope, longest of its type in the world.

68

Grizzled and gregarious, Ted DeGrazia of Tucson is a renowned Arizona artist . . . a desert original who labored as a gardener to attend the University of Arizona and whose paintings now command thirty thousand dollars. "What is your best painting?" he is asked. "The next one," he says. "I haven't painted it yet."

So rich are the Chiricahuas in life, the American Museum of Natural History established a permanent Southwestern Research Station at Portal. To this improbable oasis are attracted distinguished naturalists—from Finland, from Australia, from India. Portal residents include a dozen experts whose brain power would compliment a city of a million. Yet as they informally prowl the sky-island's hardwood canyons, they are often mistaken for ne'er-do-well prospectors. Worship of life is epitomized in a parking lot sign: "Our lizards are pets—do not molest." Around the research station one botanist counted twenty-five species of cactus and a hundred species of moss. At another small area, five hundred and seven species of eighty botanical families were found. To date, some one hundred seventy species of birds have been sighted—including six kinds of hummingbirds, ten flycatchers, twelve owls, and fourteen hawks and eagles. An ornithologist, with four hundred seventy species on his life list, observed fifty-seven species new to him during a week's stay at the research station.

"And, of course," confides a sky-islander to us, "you do know that Vladimir Nabokov spent quite a bit of time here. He wrote much of *Lolita* here, when he wasn't pursuing his hobby of butterfly collecting."

70 *Crackling with electricity and rumbling with thunder, a summer squall quarrels across Christopher Creek. Pressed northward from the Gulf of California, thundershowers are Arizona's relief following the driest months—May and June—when drought-nagged ranchers turn sunburnt masks toward a sky that withholds rain when they need it and pours it when they don't.*

CHAPTER FOUR

Rims and Forests

"Ride shotgun, if you want," says the driver of the Mogollon Stage, indicating
a seat at his right. The horsepower is mechanical, but through the rim country
of central and eastern Arizona still runs a stagecoach remindful of frontier times.

Romantic and nostalgic, the Mogollon Stage is the only public transportation between bustling, booming Phoenix and relaxed, mile-high Payson
eighty-five miles to the north. The roadsides are grazed by bald-faced steers,
and the ridges are browsed by mule deer. Indians, no longer hostile, are as
eye-catching as ever—Apaches in tall straw hats and wide squaw dresses. The
stage driver is nine-tenths cowboy, and he dresses the part.

Today's coaches are minibuses, nifty improvements over last century's
animal-drawn wagons with feedsack seats. State Highway 87 (the Beeline)
improves the rutted trail of the 1880s. Yet as before, the stage hauls ranchers
into town to borrow from the banks and brings back fetching schoolmarms
to tutor the mountain kids. Freight stuffed in corners and piled on top is barbed
wire, tractor parts, blood plasma, baby chicks, and an itinerant vaquero's saddle.
Some of the passengers are tourists who an hour ago hurtled into Phoenix in

a 747 jet, and now they unwind in a carefree adventure through an authentic remainder of a slower, earlier lifestyle.

This was the country that Zane Grey in the early 1900s chose as a favored hunting ground. By horseback, Grey followed hounds after grizzly bear and mountain lion. Between hunts, he would sit on his porch, writing in longhand, inspired by hundred-mile views. And today, although civilization has invaded the main trails through the rim country, most of it is reserved as open space national forest, with four great tracts remaining as wilderness.

Leaving Phoenix, the road to Payson is guarded by giant cacti and embellished by flowering shrubs and annuals. But soon the Mogollon Stage reaches the rolling shoulders of the Mazatzal Range. The driver calls out the place names: "Four Peaks," "Tombstone Ridge," "Screwtail Hill," "Reno Pass." Ranches here may encompass fifty thousand acres. Hereford and Angus beeves bear historic brands:

Bar Diamond ◇   Circle Bar ⊖   Cross F XF

M Bar M   Bar Tee Bar -T-

On the route is a ghost town, Cinnebar, with a shutdown mercury mine. The Mogollon Stage regularly stops midway at the Sunflower Store, where a flatland foreigner may pull on a bottle of pop while seated on a stool between a forest ranger and a cougar hunter.

Then it's back on the stage, with the driver pointing out more landmarks: "Saddleback Mountain," "Rye Creek," "Oxbow Hill," "Mazatzal Summit." The latter, in the custom of the rim country, the driver pronounces, "Mad-as-hell." As he wheels along, he waves a hand at every other car. He pitches a newspaper to a remote ranch gate. He brakes sharply to allow a covey of quail chicks to cross the road. He has a thousand stories about Mogollon Rim wildlife that he has sighted in a million miles of driving. He's logged elk, lynx, bear. And now, with the blue-gray battlements of the rim rearing in his windshield, the driver without embarrassment confesses his passionate loyalty to his realm of woods and mounts.

"I love it," he says. "My heart's here."

The rim country. By extended definition it stretches from Williams and Flagstaff in northern Arizona, in a semicircle southeastward nearly three hundred miles, deep into New Mexico. The rim is the southern abrupt edge of the Colorado Plateau, in many places seven thousand feet above sea level. Escarpments fall away for fifteen hundred feet from the rocky rim. Behind and under the rim grows America's largest continuous stand of ponderosa pine, greening granite mesas, hugging shoulders of two-lane roads and marking the

72

No longer "those damned woolies" that touched off range wars in the late nineteenth century, sheep have become acceptable co-users of the ranges of Arizona, tended by Indians and Basques on assigned allotments. This large band summering near Williams will go south to warmer pastures during winter.

municipal limits of rim-country towns. Under a cooler, wetter, bluer sky, time is measured in the syncopated creaking of a rusty windmill, and life is allowed small indulgence in abstraction. Spiritual descendants of mountain men Pauline Weaver, Ewing Young, and the Robidoux brothers, rim-country residents tend to cheerful optimism, open-door generosity, and independence bordering defiance.

The character of the driver of the Mogollon Stage has been honed by hardwood canyon and volcanic bluff. In him is embodied a bit of homesteader, wagonmaster, prospector, cavalryman, and trailherd—all of whom roved the rim country within memory of living men. Only a century or so ago, the Butterfield Overland posted a warning for its Arizona-bound passengers, "The safety of your person cannot be vouchsafed by anyone but God." Those were the days when leather-sprung "celerity" wagons, capable of carrying nine passengers inside and more on top, averaged five miles per hour for ten cents a mile. Stage robbery was commonplace; in the 1870s six passengers of the Wickenburg stage were slain by highwaymen.

But not today. The Mogollon Stage halts at the Payson station right on time. The driver grips the elbows of the ladies as they step down, and he shakes hands with every man and boy. Tossing down a suitcase, he says to a customer, "And, thanks for riding shotgun, pardner."

He is a man torn between two communities.

Phoenix—desert metropolis, city of youth, culture of climate and comfort, center of space-age industry, still more handsome than flawed, and trying to keep it that way.

Payson—mountain village, supply base for half of Gila County, a mix of lanky pulpwood cutters, weatherburnt catskinners, federal professionals, mom 'n' pop shopkeepers, sharp-nosed cabin brokers, moonlighting womenfolk, and in certain seasons, all manner of dudes from the big city down south.

"I lock my car in Phoenix because I'm afraid some stranger might steal it," says the man with divided affection. "In Payson, I leave the keys in the ignition, in case some friend will need to borrow it."

Until recently the Valley of the Sun and its satellite town were light-years apart. Driving time was five hours on a tyrannical road whose tribute was two blown-out tires and a full set of shattered nerves. Now the Beeline Highway reduces the drive to ninety minutes.

"Essentially, though, the places remain quite different," says he. "The experts in urban development recognize that Phoenix has arrived at that horrid moment in growth when too many citizens lack sense of community. The west

Rescued from ruin, Zane Grey's retreat, "Under the Tonto Rim," is lovingly restored and refurbished in original condition for public enjoyment. Grey had the cabin built as a hunting and writing lodge after the turn of the century. Abandoned for forty years, the place was rebuilt by William Goettl of Phoenix.

side only incidentally cares about the east side, which would just as soon ignore downtown. Cures and preventions of this erosion of citizenship are sought all over. Planners scrutinize Los Angeles. Officials query Washington. Maybe a convention center will help. Maybe not. Perhaps a network of freeways. Perhaps not."

And Payson is a paradise where never is heard a discouraging word?

"To the contrary. There are marvelous brawls over medicine, law enforcement, highway alignment, treatment of Indians, school financing, sewer improvements, and policies of the U. S. Forest Service, locally known as the Department of Aggravation. Citizen for citizen, Payson probably has argued with itself ten times as much as Phoenix.

"And that's the point. A healthy percentage of Payson people are intelligently attuned to local problems, and they feel they can apply leverage with their opinions. The urbanologists could learn something here; when Payson as a town was buried under a record blizzard that caved in roofs and stranded hundreds, Payson responded all for one and one for all, so long as the emergency lasted. In the same winter Phoenix was threatened by far greater dangers, which the citizenry by and large chose to ignore."

Is that all to your theory of community?

"No. Another quality Payson has, and Phoenix is losing, is civic sodality. Payson is a unit with corporate choices. One recent year, for the sheer joy of it, Payson elected Polly Brown the rodeo beauty queen. She made all the appearances and cut all the ribbons and led the parade, riding as straight as she did seventy years ago when she helped drive a herd of Texas cattle across the flooded Gila. If it wishes, Payson dances in the streets. If it so desires, it builds a clinic with volunteer workers. Can you imagine Phoenix sending a ninety-year-old Miss America candidate to Atlantic City some year?"

And is there more, man of two towns?

"I call it the integrity of eye contact. The justice reared in Payson and seen by everybody every day is a hard man to buy, and you can bet the homemade pie at the Beeline Cafe is really made at home, because the cook wouldn't know how to tell that kind of lie. Deep down, I suspect there is as much per capita greed and meanness and folly among my Payson neighbors as among my Phoenix acquaintances, but here the union of minds on common interests continues to thwart the most selfish of human urges—and that could be one definition of civilization."

Most travelers are too much in a hurry to stop in Punkin Center and admire its three attractions. The Store. The Schoolhouse. The Suspension Bridge.

Although near the middle of the state, Punkin (not Pumpkin) Center is about as far removed as possible from mainstream Arizona. Only this decade did electricity arrive to power the ice-making refrigerator in the kitchen of the area's most prominent couple, whose honeymoon in 1911 began with an all-day, sixty-mile horseback ride off the rim into Tonto Basin. The Punkin Center Store is where the mechanic's wife serves as news exchange, can opener, United Fund, anthropologist, nurse, stylesetter, and petty cashier to a clutch of customers which in any given minute might include a millionaire rancher in run-over boots, a circle of gangling cowpunchers jousting at dime-ante stud poker, and some barelegged ranch girls kibitzing. Punkin Center Store displays a five-pound Indian ax and an eight-foot bullsnake skin.

The Schoolhouse is as useful a structure to be found anywhere in the nation. It is the social, governmental, and educational bosom for a valley bigger than some eastern states, yet populated by only a hundred families, nearly all involved in raising cows. So highly regarded is the school building, twice a year every family dispatches a representative to clean and repair it, not only for the twelve to twenty pupils, who on weekdays will divide into grades around the one room, but also for the "doin's," evenings and weekends.

One night this model of multiple-use might shelter an explanation of new grazing regulations by the district ranger; next night it might reverberate to the modish beat of a teen-age dance. On a Tuesday it is polling place for a hundred voters; on a Saturday it may shelter a stork shower. Next day are Bible classes. An important wedding will attract a schoolful to sprays of wildflowers, a three-tiered cake, and pink punch in a cut-glass bowl. Not all "the doin's" are so chaste; following roundup, marathon fiddlers take over the school, and Punkin Center women spread feasts under the hackberry trees. Men one bath removed from kerosene, burnt hide, corral dust, cattle dope, and horse lather swing their partners to "The Waltz You Saved for Me" and "Trouble Among the Yearlings." If Tonto Basin cowpunchers outnumber the women, the men dance with brooms while waiting to cut in, or they stand outside in the shafts of light from the windows and reach up under their Levi's pants and produce pints of bourbon from their boot tops. Little wonder, when one year a shortage of children beclouded the Punkin Center School, a rancher imported a hired hand whose only virtue was virility: six kids.

The Suspension Bridge connects the banks of 75-mile-long Tonto Creek. Normally at Punkin Center the Tonto runs so shallow a nimble stone-hopper can cross dry-footed. But when a warm, early rain falls on the rim country snowpack, the Tonto jumps up for weeks on end—a raging yellow torrent cutting off the east side of Tonto Basin, but for the bridge. Two gnarled cottonwoods are bridge towers from which are spun random lengths and sizes of elderly, corroded scrap cable reinforced here and there with sticks of boiler tubing. Whereas other notable suspension bridges of the world have never fallen, the Punkin Center Bridge is ever on the verge of collapsing (excepting, of course, when it is collapsed).

In use, the center sways crazily and sags to a scant two feet above the maelstrom. When Dale Cline and Charlie Blake are plunged into the creek—not funny! The water is chill, head-deep, and racing, and they swim for their lives. As soon as they drain their boots and regain their breath, they are obliged to repair the bridge. The rule is, who breaks the bridge must fix it, and fix it well, for next to cross the creek are Salty and Roxie Lynn Holt and their two toddlers, ages two and one.

"Young'uns nowadays don't appreciate a modern convenience like the bridge," grumps George Cline, pioneer rancher. "In '05 when the creek was up, there wasn't a bridge and I had to get across, so I swum her. My old pony went under at midstream and I was washed out of the saddle, but I reached back and grabbed the horse's tail, and he towed me to the other side."

The Suspension Bridge. A far superior passage, even when the cables snap.

What peace. What beauty. The hiker leans back against a black walnut tree and drinks in the panorama. Flower-strewn meadow. Handsome pine forest. Nearby looms a tumbledown ranch house, with leaning walls, ruptured porch, holed roof, rotting floors. Deadwood shrouds hang in rosebushes and apple trees, and only the snap of a flycatcher and roll of distant thunder break the midday peace.

Ah, thinks the hiker, what a perfect retreat from the frantic pace and terrible pressure of modern living.

At this moment the ghost of a bearded, stooped man, dressed in wispy denim, stomps through the front door of the delapidated house. He cups his hands and shouts:

"Fraud! Phony! Faker!"

"Hey, wait a minute, Ghost," says the hiker. "Why are you yelling at me?"

"Because I'm fed up with you soft city fellers leaning against my tree and feeling sorry for yourselves."

"Well," the hiker argues, "the world seems to be moving too fast nowadays. People are under great strain. They are cracking up and burning out. They no longer have enough time to refresh themselves while coping with the awesome problems of the last third of the twentieth century."

Ghost unlooses an ethereal stream of tobacco juice into the eye of a daisy.

78

In the Snow Bowl near Flagstaff, one of several Arizona skiing areas, a downhill racer takes on the slalom.

"Haw! What makes your generation believe it inherited more than its share of tension?"

"Everybody says so," replies the hiker. "You pick up the journals or turn on television, and it's all about the conflicts of the cities, corruption of officials, and the problems of pollution. Then there's inflation and taxes and strikes and wars. And our young people think conditions have never been so bad. A lot of them want to return to the simple, unhurried, enriching life that you led, closer to nature, without being bothered with electrical appliances and central heating and mechanical aids."

Ghost laughs bitterly and says, "Let me tell you about the worries and duties of my day. I got up before first light and made the fire and hauled water and milked the cow. I fed stock and slopped hogs and chopped wood. I hitched the team and plowed a field and mended fence.

"I planted crops. Hoed weeds. Trapped wolves and fought bears that carried off my calves. I harvested, if the drought and bugs left anything to harvest, and then I took my crops to market, if and when there was a market.

"My woman baked bread and canned vegetables and crocked eggs. She churned butter, filled lamps, carried ashes, ground coffee, killed snakes, and scrubbed clothes. She grew old before her time.

"We had a 12 per cent mortgage at the bank, and a big bill at the store in town, and no cash. And no government check or welfare department between us and starving to death. Do you believe that nature is a benevolent old gal? Why, one year we were burned out by a forest fire started by lightning, and the next year we lost our barn in a flood because there wasn't a dam.

"We watched our youngsters taken by diseases that didn't have names, let alone cures. Those that survived had to work like slaves and miss out on education beyond the three Rs."

"But, Ghost," pleads the hiker, "ours is a complex society. You lived in the golden age of the independent Westerner. Maybe you didn't have power or motorized tools or modern home conveniences, or wonder drugs or rapid communication and transportation, or education and cultural entertainment, but what of your simple pleasures? Your gratifying rewards? Your moments of tranquil reflection?"

Ghost jeers, "In forty years I never had a minute to sit down under that walnut tree. Now git off'n my place!"

These days big-time cowboy tournaments are diluted by circus acts and glittering balladeers. At Heber, at other towns on and under the rim, at forty places around the state of Arizona, rodeo flourishes in its purest forms—riding,

Blue Ridge Lake on East Clear Creek. Mogollon Rim country, north of Payson.

Among better beef herds of Arizona are those of the White Mountain Apaches, here in the midst of roundup near Whiteriver. Highly successful in tribal enterprises, Apaches today run a showcase sawmill, live in newly built subdivisions, and welcome (for a slight fee) non-Indians to camp and fish along a score of lakes and three hundred miles of trout streams.

Fields of gold, Apache National Forest.

Under The Totem Pole and other spires of Monument Valley, Navajos tend a flock of their economically important sheep. Of Arizona's hundred thousand Indians, largest tribe is the Navajo, whose links to Asia include birthmarks, epicanthic eyes, and similarities of language.

Spectrum of autumn, Coconino National Forest.

Cloud shadows undulate across ponderosa forests under the Mogollon Rim, dominant physical feature of central Arizona. The view is to Tonto National Forest, one of the ten most popular recreation areas in the national forest system.

In an upside-down quirk of whimsical nature, the saturated volcanic muds of an ancient era have become the superdry Chinle formation of the Painted Desert of northeastern Arizona.

Bronze buttes and frowning rims frame Oak Creek Falls in a canyon second only to Grand Canyon in popularity with recreationists.

Never without a touch of snow are the San Francisco peaks north of Flagstaff, rising to 12,670 feet above sea level. Volcanic in origin, the mountains support an area of arctic tundra and specimens of the oldest living things on earth: bristlecone pines. Arizona bristlecones are as old as fifteen hundred years, and some specimens in California were living before Moses led his people to the Promised Land.

roping, and wrestling. And rightly so, inasmuch as Prescott (or maybe Payson) sponsored America's first organized rodeo in the 1880s. At Heber, not much has changed. The spectators stuffed with barbecue waddle over to the arena of a late Saturday afternoon. Get on with it, they holler. Families park vehicles for seats along the fence and up among the limestone towers that intrude on the clearing. Girls perch on the corral rails. The announcer has no need of a loudspeaker; he has learned in northern Arizona to talk against the wind. For Heber, it is Mardi Gras, Super Bowl, and Coronation Week.

The rodeo begins on impulse, with a grand entrance of the American flag, three princesses, and a thundering posse of contestants. Several are ninety-pound lads, and a few are seventy-year codgers. After a wild-cow race, the entrants take up serious work—calf roping, bull riding, horse racing, barrel bending, and team tying. Impelled by a sense of tradition they risk their necks for unworthy rewards in contests of intense brutality. The stock is dangerously unpredictable. As a cowboy testifies, "I run down the rope lookin' fer the critter and met him a-comin' up the rope lookin' fer me." But heck, Frank Condon once rode a bull bison in Prescott. Jim Carter used to give steers a hundred-foot head start. John deGraffenried one day rode an outlaw bronc into a Pearce barbershop for a $25 prize. Everett Bowman bulldogged steers on Payson's main street before moving on to Madison Square Garden. Pete Haverty had but one leg, but he rode broncs and roped steers. So come on, Heber, get on with it.

A ton of furious, red-eyed bull is matched against a slim, show-off cowboy. One jump. Two. The half-Brahman brute has breakfasted on bedsprings. It swaps ends, snorts and rears. And before anyone fully grasps the action, the bull is mincing at the far end of the arena, and the man is flat, ashen, and still in the black dirt. The fellow doesn't waken for a quarter of an hour, and as they carry him away to the hospital he waves feebly to the cheering crowd.

"The only way you can kill a bull rider," avers the announcer, "is to cut off his head and bury it where he can't find it. So let's get on with it, folks."

Father and daughter, we rest on a stump four feet in diameter and review a perfect day. We hiked the high forest at a pace to sense its rhythms. In the death and decay of last year's leaves, bacteria thrive. Insects rise from the ferment. Fungi barter in carbon atoms. We studied the adaptation of the porcupine and of the dappled fawn. We sniffed the mountain lilac and wood violets and wild geranium. Thrushes in courtship scandalized the next-door wrens. We chased a yellow swallowtail and spooned up a salamander from his muddy lair. And now our fingers rub the weathered braille of growth rings of the stump.

"I'd guess it was logged in the 1930s, when I was a boy."

Near its source under the Mogollon Rim, Tonto Creek forms a stride-wide falls above a pool teeming with rainbow trout. By the time Tonto joins the Gila River seventy-five miles to the south it will form a major arm of Roosevelt Lake, key reservoir for the Salt River Project's water-storage and hydroelectric-power system.

"Long before I was born."

"Did you ever think of these old stumps as history books?"

"I'm not very good at history."

We count the rings, outlined by yellow crystals of pitch. In half an inch we regress to 1927 when Charles Lindbergh nearly crashed his plane in Arizona, en route to his solo flight across the Atlantic.

"Hey, neat," says she. "Let's count some more."

In 1916, the entire Mexican border a few hundred miles from this tree was on the alert for Pancho Villa. Four inches of rings reach 1912, the year of Arizona statehood. The width of two fingers more and the Rough Riders from Arizona are charging up San Juan Hill. One foot from the perimeter, Cochise is being buried under the oaks in the Dragoon Mountains. The rings vary in thickness, indicating differences in weather from year to year. Although rare, pines four hundred years old have been cut in Arizona. In forest headquarters is a tree section dating to 1758.

On we count. In 1873, Mormon immigrants conquer the Painted Desert to settle along the Little Colorado. An inch farther, the first territorial delegate, Charles Poston, leaves for Washington. The span of a hand, Mexico cedes most of Arizona and much of the West to the United States.

The tree is a thigh-thick bole when Mexico wins independence from Spain. In 1790, of four million Americans, fewer than a hundred thousand live west of the Alleghenies. The Bill of Rights takes effect in 1791, and the core of this tree is a strong straight sapling then, surrounded by fastness. The counting passes the Articles of Confederation and Saratoga and ends at the center.

"If we've not miscounted, and our estimate of the logging year is correct, this tree germinated in 1776, the year of the Declaration of Independence. We've seen it under glass in the National Archives in Washington."

And as we two stroll homeward in the rim country, we notice the earth is covered once again by winged pine seeds.

CHAPTER FIVE

Sculptured Mesas, Painted Plains

Timidly a ten-year-old boy crawls toward the edge of Toroweap Point in Grand Canyon National Monument. He peeps down the three-thousand-foot parapet and beyond to the ribbon of river. Later, in the Park Service log he proudly writes his name, and the remark, "Today I spit a mile."

The youngster's awe-bravado symbolizes a typical, dual response to that part of the Colorado Plateau which dominates the northern quarter of Arizona. Sensitive beings are at once smaller, and larger, than ever. What place on earth so mercilessly dwarfs physical man and at the same time appeals to "the Thee in Me who works behind the Veil."

Clare Boothe Luce dubbed it, "The Land of the Long Eyes"—this sight-straining triangle of tables, steppes, and prairies bounded by Nevada, Utah, and New Mexico. Perception exceeding normal vision is helpful, when on a dull day Vermillion Cliffs vibrate with an inner incandescence. To drive a pickup truck along Uinkaret Plateau is one experience; the other dimension is to draw away to some high place and watch the truck's futile plume traverse the lonely mesa and disappear under a wart on the toe of a foothill of Mount Trumbull.

85

When sheets of silt-reddened flood abruptly cascade across the normally dry terraces of the Grand Falls of the Little Colorado River, a witness is doubly appreciative, aware that the spectacle may last ten minutes and not be repeated for a year or more. No combination of pity-envy quite compares to that felt for the Navajo family occupying a fifty-dollar house, with a million-dollar view of Monument Valley. Is the tycoon on the porch of his city mansion richer? He who never squints against unfiltered sun or breathes air like wine or cocks an ear to silence more insistent than trumpets?

By air, Bundyville is a hundred miles from its county seat. By road, the distance is 414 miles. For Bundyville is deep within the geographical oddity nicknamed "The Strip," that portion of Arizona lying north of the gorges of the Colorado River. Even into the last quarter of the twentieth century, The Arizona Strip is tied to the rest of the state by just three bridges, one of them for people and pack mules in the very bottom of Grand Canyon. All around The Strip the greatest migration in the history of man implies a Westward Tilt toward Southern California, but the sparsely populated Strip seems to be getting emptier. Years ago there were fifty farm and ranch kids and three teachers at the Bundyville school, and now there aren't enough pupils to qualify for state funds and the white frame school with the bell in the peak huddles empty and alone, all that remains of Bundyville. Today if all the people of The Strip were evenly spaced, each would stand two miles apart.

Technically, the Strip takes in the densely forested Kaibab Plateau and a shore of Lake Powell bustling with the boat crowd. But when natives say "out on the Strip" they mean that portion west of Fredonia, by nature a waterless waste that with a few wet years tricked Mormon homesteaders into foredoomed attempts at dry farming. Then they turned to grazing cattle and sheep, which stripped away the land's thin shield of grasses. As a consequence, once-gentle swales are cruelly gullied. The ranch house at Wolf Hole is abandoned as if the owners dried up and blew away. Despite imaginative efforts to inflate postage-stamp sales (a cedar fence post was mailed as a gift to John Wayne), Tuweep lost its post office anyway. The only gasoline for sale in a sixty-five-mile radius is by means of a steel drum and relic hand pump installed in self-defense at the entrance to the Craig Ranch, where they not only haul fuel for ill-prepared tourists but, during bad drought, their own domestic water from town. With hard lessons learned, most Strip residents now cluster in small communities along the Utah line. They saw logs into boards, grow hay and lucerne grass, join in community enterprises dating to early experiments in Utopian colonies, provide nearly all their own services, and coldly withdraw from any outsider's

86

Far from extinct, buffalo roam Arizona's Houserock Valley in the Strip Country north of the Colorado. A successful experiment in enlightened game management, the herd of American bison has thrived since being taken into the custody of the Arizona State Department of Game and Fish in 1927.

inquiry about home institutions. It is said that some of the men in and around Colorado City, members of a splinter sect excommunicated from the Church of Jesus Christ of Latter-day Saints, still practice polygamy. Although, God be the judge, supporting one wife has ever been a struggle in the Arizona Strip.

No more does the chocolate Colorado River boil unchallenged down its boulder-strewn race to the sea; no longer do the river runners cast their fragile craft down Powell's "carved walls, royal arches, glens, alcove gulches, mounds, and monuments" of Glen Canyon. Gray ooze claims the cleft where lobelia and columbine and maidenhair fern once delighted an explorer. Gloom hides the skeletons of sun-nurtured oaks. Where the chipmunk darted, a bass spawns. Since the middle 1960s, all is drowned, by Lake Powell.

"When they dammed up the river," says Art Greene, "the best part inside of me died." Yet he lives, at this writing, a remarkably alert octogenarian who converted unwanted, revolutionary change into a multimillion-dollar enterprise. If one person may serve as a lens for human interpretation of the river and the canyon and the lake and their wonders, he is Art Greene.

A rough gem, Greene. A foot-loose Colorado cowboy in 1910, he was among the first dozen white men to gaze upon Rainbow Bridge, premier natural arch of the plateau country. Greene had to ride a good horse a hard day through twenty miles of the wildest ground remaining in the United States. For a long time Greene was a member of one of the world's most exclusive travel clubs . . . those who had seen Rainbow.

Even though Rainbow Bridge National Monument was established in 1913, fewer than three thousand persons reached it by the mid-1920s. The hike and horse ride were never shorter than fourteen miles. By boat, the trips were at best unforgettable adventures, and at worst, fatal accidents. Seldom a year passed without a drowning in Glen Canyon. "I never lost a customer," Greene asserts, "but I never felt justified in collecting my fee in advance."

From base camp at Marble Canyon, it was a four-hundred-mile roundabout portage to Hite, Utah, where boats could be launched. Then it was another hundred miles of treacherous river with eleven white-water rapids to the side canyon leading to Rainbow. The hike from the river wound seven miles through narrows barricaded by rock debris.

Greene charted a daring route, upriver seventy miles *against the current* from Lee's Ferry, in the late 1940s and 1950s. He tried all sorts of power, both inboard and outboard, and finally subdued Big Red with a water-spider raft pushed by a propeller, driven by a fighter plane engine. Governors and cabinet officers and movie stars were Greene's guests then. Without complaint they accepted

As if applauding its own botanical exhibits, Monument Valley raises a Mitten, one of a pair of hand-shaped formations shared by Arizona and Utah.

Sentinel at entrance to
Monument Valley is
(as Kit Carson called it)
El Capitan or (as the
Navajo prefer) Agathla
Needle. Well over a mile high,
the igneous needle marks the
place where, by Navajo lore,
the old people gathered to
process antelope hides.

Not long ago beyond reach of all but the most intrepid explorers, the Glen Canyon country is penetrated by a million fingers of man-made Lake Powell—186 miles of artificial inland sea. When Europeans first came to Arizona, only one lake existed—tiny Stoneman Lake at the bottom of a collapsed volcano—and today the state has dozens of impoundments providing power, recreation, and sometimes controversy in a time of environmental second thoughts.

92

the heat and cold, the moldy sleeping bags and sandy pancakes, and Art Greene's elfish devotion to pure democracy. Once he guided a family of famous photographers up Glen Canyon, and throughout the journey, Greene insisted that a nine-year-old boy have equal vote in every decision.

River people soon learn to live one day for itself. The past has vanished around a bend; the swift current will deliver the future soon enough. Life is now; no disaster of yesterday should mar the present. One time a customer, an elderly man, asked Greene to stop at the wreck of an antique dredge.

"He gathered up a few pieces of driftwood and he built a fire and put on a pot of coffee," says Art. "There were three of us, and he poured out three cups of coffee, and he said, 'Boys, I hope you enjoy this as much as I do. Long ago I spent $75,000 on this dredge, and before she could wash out an ounce of gold, the river wrecked her. Did you ever drink a $25,000 cup of coffee'?"

As late as 1960, the number of visitors to Rainbow totaled no more than ten thousand. Meanwhile, to the anguish of nature lovers, Glen Canyon Dam rose between the vertical walls of Navajo sandstone at Page. Inevitably, Greene's livelihood would be threatened. Although bearing enough years to turn lesser men elderly, Greene led his family on scouting expeditions for a particular parcel of land, high out on the rugged slopes northwest of the damsite. They hammered up some cabins, caught rain water, and generally earned a reputation among the dam builders as "that loco Greene bunch." But when the waters began backing behind the dam, and the government called for concession bids, there, first in line, stood Art Greene, sun-cured, tobacco-scorched, and brandishing an ironclad lease on the most attractive future recreational shore.

By the mid-1960s Greene and his family began transporting sight-seers, including the feeble and crippled, to Rainbow and back in a day, in fast, snug cabin cruisers with all the conveniences. The rising lake reduced the walk to the bridge to a few hundred yards. And of a recent year the Greene boats carried more than eleven thousand people to Rainbow—for that first glimpse of salmon stone wider than a football field and taller than the nation's capitol. Still more thousands passed through the Wahweap Marina to fish and ski and motor on a man-made body of water so enormous it measurably bends the earth's crust and alters downwind weather patterns. For all that is lost, Powell created a shoreline longer than the nation's west coast.

"Everything's changed," says Art Greene. "Nothing in all that country is the same as it was in the beginning."

Nine hundred feet straight down, the skirt of the resting Navajo woman scribes a radiant purple circle against the tawny floor of Canyon de Chelly.

Her dingy sheep mill all around her. Up canyon, her man spurs his horse after strays, mere nits beneath towering maroon bluffs and brooding thunderheads. A daughter romps after a dog down a rippled dune.

White passengers from four tour buses stand along the rim of the Spider Rock overlook and absorb the singular setting. Four hundred Navajos migrate every summer to guard their flocks, plant crops, and tend orchards within the fortress walls of sacred canyons. The whites look down and wonder. What do they know of the Navajo? The whites vaguely concede that Navajos are artistically refined but hopelessly quaint. They are subarctic Athabascans who subsist on mutton and soda pop. They hide in their heads patterns for strong, colorful rugs. They are masterful with silver and horses.

Never were they defeated in a war, by Spaniard, by Mexican, by American. In 1863 Kit Carson's cavalry drummed into de Chelly and warred against sheep, horses, and three thousand fruit trees. Only then, at the brink of starvation, did half the tribe submit to the Long Walk to a promised paradise at Bosque Redondo, New Mexico.

There, the land was salty. Corn withered. Livestock perished. Comanche, Mexican, and Anglo bandits raided the settlements, and disease decimated the survivors. Over a period of five years, two thousand Navajos died. At last, Lieutenant General William T. Sherman came to make treaty, to hear the pleas of Navajo chiefs. Barboncito . . . sick, hungry, impoverished . . . spoke directly to him who put the torch to Georgia: "I hope to God you will not ask me to go to any country except my own. . . . I would like to go back the same road we came. . . . After we get back to our country it will brighten up again and the Navajo will be as happy as the land, black clouds will rise and there will be plenty of rain, corn will grow in abundance and everything look happy."

The prayer was answered, and the Navajos returned, many to the vicinity of Canyon de Chelly, ultimate sanctuary of *Dineh*—The People. When the Great White Father again sought to take Canyon de Chelly, as a national monument, the Navajos insisted on a one-of-a-kind arrangement. The Park Service could have administrative jurisdiction over the hundreds of prehistoric sites, but the Navajos would continue to own the land, with freedom to graze their livestock and harvest their replanted peach trees. And every white man setting foot inside de Chelly would do so as an alien.

Thus, the Navajos have managed a better bargain with Canyon de Chelly than did the Pueblo people displaced by the Navajo. The extraordinary archaeological treasures of de Chelly predate the Navajos' arrival and indicate human occupation as early as A.D. 348. These, too, were besieged peoples. The nomadic Basket Makers and their descendants excelled at potmaking and corn planting.

An intruding race of flatheads brought cotton and the bow and arrow to de Chelly, and they clustered together for protection. The Early Pueblo cultures saw rise of personal and public wealth—beads and trinkets and hoards of grain. Their homes doubled as forts.

The great Pueblo Period extended beyond through A.D. 1200 and flowered in Canyon de Chelly (as at Mummy Cave) with three-story, ninety-room apartment houses. The undercut Defiance Plateau provided building sites protected from weather, long after the original inhabitants vanished. As a scientist wrote of his work in 1927, "No diggings, at least in the Southwest, can compare with it in interest. For among the trash of straw and twigs and cornhusks that make up the body of the deposit are literally thousands of specimens of perishable nature, never found in ancient sites that have been exposed to weather. Sandals, leatherwork, textiles, basketry, wooden implements, forgotten caches of corn, broken toys; all preserved so perfectly and all carrying so vivid a human interest that one develops a feeling of intimacy with the old people." At Battle Cove was unearthed the mummy of "the Weaver," wrapped in a blanket woven of the breast feathers of the golden eagle and in sheets of spun cotton. His people must have revered the Weaver, for along with baskets and bowls of food, he was buried with *three miles* of yarn to busy his fingers in a nether world.

No surrealist could contrive a more enigmatic scene than this at Canyon de Chelly. Hulking Black Mountain to the southwest. Chasms through red, yellow, and gray sandstone. Cliffs, pinnacles, domes. Walls streaked with water-stain abstractions. Bold green gobs of cottonwood groves. Cliff dwellings predating Christ. Faint tracks through sand. A woman in a purple dress who believes her ancestors fired the Sun by igniting a turquoise stone. On the rim, bus tourists whose sons go to the Moon.

Among the easternmost of the badlands known as the Painted Desert is dispersed the largest exposure of petrified wood in the world. Even so, the supply may not be enough to prevent an adoring public from picking the area clean. The Petrified Forest could become the first National Park packed home by America, bit by bit.

Could, that is, if it weren't for the Park Service rangers who every day foil some citizen's impulse to cop a souvenir. Contraband petrified wood has been detected in bikini bathing suits, in baby diapers, under garters, in hairdos, and behind dashboards. As nowhere else in the park system, say the rangers, their roles conflict. They are expected to be cheerful, informative hosts. And simultaneously they are the rules keepers for more than a million visitors a year—each a potential pirate.

The place is barren enough, as is. Sparsely vegetated and dramatically dismantled, wherever the eye wanders, the wastes are dotted with petrified wood, in sizes from pebbles to entire logs.

The stony wood indeed began as trees, mainly a kind of tall pine that grew a hundred eighty million years ago when local reptiles were eighteen feet long and salamanders had three eyes. Probably a flood felled the forest, carried it eastward, and buried it in the clayish soil of the Chinle formation. Pressurized underground, minerals displaced the wood cells. Rainbow colors were imparted by traces of iron, manganese, copper, and chromium. Much later, when the land was lifted and stripped away, this forest of semiprecious gems was exposed to view.

To mankind's credit, today's petty thievery is nothing to practices of the past. Prehistoric Indians used jeweled logs as building blocks; Agate House is a conspicuous example. Jewel-like arrowheads were flaked from petrified wood. The West and its splendors seemed inexhaustible to early explorers and settlers. Stone tree trunks were freighted away. Jewelers blasted logs seeking jasper, agate, and amethyst. Many a pioneer tourist fetched home a sparkling doorstop. A stamp mill was being erected for crushing the logs into abrasives, when in 1906 President Roosevelt withdrew the forest from public misuse.

In their preferred roles as guides, the park rangers today encourage longer visits. Good roads off Interstate 40 and U. S. 60 abet superficial motor tours. The average tourist zips through in two hours, compelled to hurry on to the next "Gas Food" or "Rest Stop" down the freeway. More rewarding are hikes along trails up and down gentle slopes. Newspaper Rock, etched by Indian picture-writing, can be seen up close, and Agate Bridge, a hundred-foot-long log spanning a forty-foot-deep wash, is where Tom Paine, a Hashknife cowboy, won a ten-dollar bet by galloping his horse across in 1886.

The yen for a petrified keepsake need not be stifled altogether. Outside the park at curio shops, petrified wood gathered from private land is for sale for as little as five cents per sample. This is much less expensive than the experience of a California woman who somehow shoplifted a park boulder weighing forty-seven pounds. Her conscience nagged her, so she returned the stone via parcel post.

In common with Grand Canyon, Monument Valley strikes people in unpredictable personal terms. To some, the rearing rock formations are exclamation points upon a promise of eternity. To others, they seem as scarred and useless as motel dressers. But nobody in their presence can ignore them.

The setting is mind-boggling—a vast depression into the mile-high plateau

Pantheon of gods of the Navajo people, Monument Valley displays its ethereal mood.

Sunset at Grand Canyon from South Rim.

South Rim, as seen from North Rim of Grand Canyon.

Angel's window, North Rim, Grand Canyon.

Point Imperial, North Rim, Grand Canyon.

Cape Royal, North Rim, Grand Canyon.

Nonnezosheboko (Great Arch), the Navajo calls it, and in this aerial photograph it is left of center near the bottom. So effective in placing man puny in comparison, the 309-foot-high arch is in turn reduced by the convoluted masses surrounding it.

Pyramid Arch, Mystery Valley, a part of Monument Valley.

Window Rock is name-giving feature of Navajo capital. Largest of the surviving American tribes, the Navajo live in a reservation the size of West Virginia, rich in oil, coal, timber, and recreational resources. The people are young: median age, 17. So complex is their language, Navajo radio operators during World War II communicated Navy secrets openly in their native tongue, a code the Japanese could never break. At Window Rock are evidences of the new Navajo: a chicken-to-go restaurant, an electronics plant, and a million-dollar motel with a card next to room telephones: T'aa yedigo adeli'i. (We try harder.)

country. Comb Reef on the south and east strains to roll for thirty miles and crash against Hoskinini Mesa on the west, or surge northward for sixty miles to plunge into the San Juan River.

Preposterous imagery? Forces no less prodigious created Monument Valley. Sandstones hardened beneath an ancient ocean until seventy million years ago when, at about the time of the upheaval of the Rocky Mountains, this region lifted up, folded, and shattered. Volcanos added plugs and dikes of granite. As landmarks rose, the counterforces of erosion labored: the wind worrying a grain of sand; an ounce of water freezing and splitting a boulder; a colony of lichen dissolving minerals with chemicals. These and the greater powers, torrent, gale, avalanche, flood, continue to expose the briny origins of this land. Fossils of shellfish and footprints of amphibians are everywhere imbedded in the solidified sediment. After a rain shower, an unmistakable scent of salt spray perfumes the air.

Not all of the incredible formations and features are named. There are natural bridges, sand spouts, windows, caves, echo chambers. The Totem Pole. The Mittens. Three Sisters. Ear of the Wind. The Camel. Eye of the Sun. Arrogant man's temporary labels on spires forty-five stories tall; on a valley where mirages dance around the horizons and optical illusions warp perspective. It is a mystical place, home of supernatural spirits, or so believe the Navajo Indians who dwell beneath the monuments.

To many a non-Indian, also, Monument Valley is a holy place—an open-air cathedral where guilt and confession and dogma are quite beside the point. Men count minutes; the monuments ignore millenniums. Amid nonsectarian temples each worshiper communes with the deities of his faith. The time of baptism is sundown, when the valley catches fire and ignites the sky. Shadows accelerate. The monuments glow in pink and ochre and scarlet. White Shell Woman (the Moon) waits in a hogan far across the western ocean, and the Sun hurries to make love to her. In that moment, out in a darkling canyon, a Navajo medicine man chants "The Song of Talking God."

> *With goodness and beauty before me I go;*
> *With goodness and beauty behind me I go;*
> *With goodness and beauty above me I go;*
> *With goodness and beauty below me I go;*
> *With goodness and beauty in all things*
> *around me I go;*
>
> *Thus being I, I go.*

Navajo medicine men and women are officially accepted as healers by the state of Arizona, and their rites are kept fresh for every step in life—puberty, sickness, return from battle. The recitation of just one ceremony, the Mountain Way, used in treatment of epilepsy, requires the equivalent in white culture of memorizing completely the Episcopal Book of Common Prayer. The rite lasts nine days, with five hundred songs of twelve verses each.

CHAPTER SIX

Many Tongues, Many Nations

Accustomed to rolling farms and hardwood hollows of Virginia, I recoiled from the thrifty scrubs and jagged horizons of the Gila River Indian Reservation. More unsettling, for the first time in my fourteen years I was a member of a minority race and resident of a community of the poor. Instead of painted bungalows and paved streets, all about were boxy hovels of mud and sticks containing ruddy people whose speech seemed flawed by glottal stops and fricatives. No Blue Ridge flora camouflaged the squalor of Sacaton, the capital of the Pima Nation, in the early 1940s. One water spigot served a neighborhood; rickety backhouses uglified junky yards; drought and neglect blighted dusty, weedy fields. Many of the adults seemed broken in spirit.

Back East I'd held rank and tenure in one of the nation's oldest, richest Boy Scout troops, with a permanent camp of its own in the hills, a locker crammed with equipment, every member fully uniformed. Now, that, too, was lost. Unknowingly, I was something of a deliverance for Sacaton's graying Presbyterian missionary. Given a scout of experience to share leadership, he obtained a scout troop charter. With misgivings, I agreed to go along with the experiment. There had never been Pima scouts, other than those with the Army during Apache wars.

From the outset, certain ideals of the scouting movement conflicted with Sacaton realities. Saving money for uniforms was impossible for lads whose parents might not see more than a few hundred dollars in a year. Teachings from the white boy handbook ricocheted off Pima skulls. But afield, the Indian youths camped with the easy grace of born woodsmen and howled at their leader, slung in a hammock above the fangs of imagined rattlesnakes. Yet across the ethnocentric barriers lore was exchanged; the Indians accepted the formalities of Lord Baden-Powell; by the hour I listened to the legends of Elder Brother and Little Yellow Bird, and even learned some Pima. An appreciation flourished for a people who once were so industrious they could sell millions of pounds of surplus grain to white American travelers, and yet by 1872 were close to starvation. During Saguaro Harvest Moon our troop journeyed by school bus around Arizona, the state with fourteen tribes on nineteen reservations and more Indians than any other state in the nation. We swam naked (as Indians) in mountain lakes, slept on awesome rims, and, as racially different youngsters may when allowed to, became lifelong friends.

Came an invitation. Catalina Council would hold its annual camporee off the Pima reservation east of Sacaton. Would the newest troop like to tag along and learn the ropes of big-time camping competition? The scoutmaster was willing. My old doubts returned, in recalling past camporees: the strict procedures, the constant judging. But Sacaton was pillaged of a ragbag assortment of equipment, a tent fly from the cotton research station, some holey blankets from the mission, pots and pans from the Indian school.

Like a guerrilla auxiliary, Troop 14 jumped off a cattle truck onto the campground outside Coolidge. Here were the aloof, affluent troops from Tucson, and other urban centers, unpacking pressed uniforms, setting up new tents, unrolling kapok bedrolls on air mattresses. The Indian boys made the most of what they had. They dug hip holes for unpadded beds of tarps and blankets. For perishables they contrived a desert cooler of moistened burlap, copied after those at home. Rather than coop up in airless tents, they roofed a *ramada* that welcomed cooling breezes from any direction. Their meals were ears of corn roasted whole in mesquite coals, while city scouts opened cans. Fire builders for their families, the Pima boys brought their gallon of water to a rolling boil before most of the white troops fanned flame in tinder. Grandsons of Army scouts, Troop 14 raced through the tracking contest while their white competitors lost the trail. At ceremonies on the final day, a gruff scout executive with a faint smile pinned the camporee championship streamer to Troop 14's flag.

Spinning yarn, a contemporary Navajo woman remains tied by custom and belief to the past. "They are fervently religious," says Arizona's Senator Barry M. Goldwater, long-time student of the Navajo. "They are highly intelligent, witty, and shy. And, basically, they do not respect the white man. . . . In their scale of values, the Navajo is at the very top, next come the other races, and at the bottom, the white man. I suspect it will take a long time before the white man gets any higher."

Hopi dancers and singers at Flagstaff Pow Wow keep time to gourd rattles and bear brightly colored ceremonial plaques.

Of natural fibers tinted with native dyes, a Hopi woman weaves a basket that may become a gift, a means of barter, or an athlete's trophy.

With no more to guide her than a mental image, a Navajo weaver works her simple loom. Today a Two Gray Hills rug the size of a saddle blanket might command $3,000, and still the weaver is not rich. Her portion is $1,500 for eighteen months of weaving, not counting her labors in raising sheep, shearing, cleaning, carding, and spinning, all by hand. So durable is her product that at the Chicago World's Fair four million people walked across a Navajo rug without damaging it.

. . . Thirty years sped by, and recently I returned to Sacaton for *Mul-cha-tha,* "a gathering of the people for festivities." At rodeo chutes, around crafts shops, at the stands selling beans and fry bread were familiar faces, older and rounder, but undefeated.

"You wouldn't recognize the old reservation," said one. "The Arts and Crafts Center is completed off Interstate 5. Our land is strategically positioned between the industrial expansions of Phoenix and Tucson. Three of our own industrial parks are producing everything from mobile homes to canvas tents. That's right, *tents.* Our people are employed as key-punch operators and other skilled workers right here on the reservation. We're into all sorts of projects— adult education, a career-training center, an artificial lake with a timed speed course. We're farming twenty thousand acres under Pima managers. And we're in charge. For too long a time, government agencies *dictated to* the Pimas, and now we insist on the last word in every long-term plan. A new day comes for the Pima."

He said emphatically, "*Vh-thaw-hup-ju.*" It *will* happen.

They are at once the most interesting and least fathomed of Americans, they who were here in the beginning. Far from vanishing, the first Americans are 800,000—as many as lived at the time of Columbus. Some two hundred sixty tribes occupy nearly three hundred reservations, although many dwell in the nation's cities. Fifteen per cent live in Arizona. On or off their reserves they vote, pay taxes, own land, can hold any office, face military obligation, buy liquor except where local option prohibits, and enjoy (by law, at least) all the civil rights of other races. Health, education, life expectancy, employability are said to be improving by the Bureau of Indian Affairs, itself an agency 50 per cent staffed by Americans of Indian blood.

For all of the curiosity they generate, American Indians suffer preposterous stereotyping. Especially in the West, despite centuries of European pressure,

Concentrating on a symbolic pattern is a Hopi weaving a narrow prayer shawl. In the Hopi tribe, men do the weaving.

Irrepressible good humor of Josephine Harrison is characteristic of her Yavapai Sun People, of Yuman stock, who once claimed a desert-to-mountain wilderness embracing twenty thousand square miles of central Arizona. Mrs. Harrison is one of the more skilled in weaving traditional baskets of coiled split willow and devil's-claw.

acculturation largely is unsuccessful, and the debates on assimilation rage most heatedly among Indians themselves. The factors of division—tribal loyalty, native religion, economic attitudes—are endless. It's difficult to imagine a greater cultural distance than that between a Four Corners Navajo elder, who has never heard a word of English, and the Navajo girl valedictorian of the Indian school set beneath the newest skyscrapers of Phoenix. At a time of widespread review of national goals and lifestyles, early Indian attitudes toward environment are beginning to gain in favor, to the dismay of "progressive" Indians who long ago adopted all the hustle and materialism of the white man's way.

Thus, there is no one *Indian question;* rather, there are 800,000 individuals of varying backgrounds, needs, and wishes. To know one is not to understand another, and the non-Indian who blithely presumes that his own society is the superior center of the family of man will gain a few insights into his red brothers.

Point and counterpoint: Researching the Mandans, a tribe of Indians of blue eyes, light skin, and blond hair, a white man asked an Arizona Hopi, "Could it have been that the Mandans were started by the Welsh or Norse or some other white race?" The Hopi replied, "Has it ever occurred to you that possibly the Mandans sailed overseas and started the white race and came back?"

December sleet draped the trading post's eaves and glazed the deserted road forks. Bob, the Papago clerk, glowered at the gloom engulfing an Indian reservation twice as big as Delaware. "Last summer our cows died of thirst," he grumped. "Now the roads are rivers. Gettin' slick. Gonna snow."

"Then please go home early," urged the trader, Peggy Kater. Usually after dark she could expect customers at all hours, from as far away as fifty miles. But not tonight. In such foul weather the Papago gods themselves hid in their underground maze. Alone, Mrs. Kater took up a cherished chore: stuffing hundreds of stockings for her Christmas party.

Abruptly, the banshee storm burst through the doorway and deposited a Papago family, blinking against the electric light. The young mother hefted an infant on her hip. Two barefoot boys left sodden tracks across the floor. The boys stared at the sweets. Mrs. Kater handed them a taste.

"Your shoes? Did you forget them?"

"*Petatcho* shoes." No shoes. Money only for "necessities."

The Papago woman without looking up explained that this winter the men of the Bean People could find no work on the reservation. Her family had traveled north to the white man's cotton fields. But the rain had ruined the

110

A rare sight in the 1970s—Papago wood gatherers in a mule-drawn, iron-tired wagon at San Xavier del Bac Mission. More likely, these days, family transportation is by pickup truck.

picking, and now they were hitchhiking back to their clay-and-cactus house at Hotason Vo.

Impulsively Mrs. Kater pulled down two new outfits from her shelves. Flannel shirts. Levi's pants. Wool socks. Quilted jackets. And shoes. The boys tensed under the white woman's touch, but they submitted to the fittings. They stroked the imitation-fur collars. Mrs. Kater prattled on to bridge the awkwardness. By a wall of horse collars the Indian mother wept in the cup of her hand. Papagos are a proud people who care for their own—when they can. The lessons of the harsh desert and the parables of the Old Ones encourage a society of sharing. To give is humankind's noblest virtue. The philosophy made the Papago the most friendly people throughout history toward their European invaders, and as a result, the Bean People were the last tribe to be granted a reservation by the Great White Father.

"No charge for the clothes," said Mrs. Kater. "Now what are your necessities?"

In the early days the Papago father with much ritual might have got *on* (salt) from the sloughs of the Sea of Cortez, a hundred miles to the south. Now he ordered a blue cylinder of *on*. Twenty-five pounds *chewey* (flour), four pounds *monjic* (lard), and a can of *espowla* (baking soda). For the tortillas, a sack of *moo* (pinto beans). For the beans, a slab of *chewhook* (fat beef). And a box of .22-caliber cartridges for rabbit hunting. Each item was ordered and purchased separately so that the remaining money might be measured against priorities. Through the complicated negotiating, Peggy Kater babbled on, the living newspaper of the reservation. The weather might worsen. So-and-so got married. What's-his-name is sick.

"Remember the party," she said. "The kids are invited." And she idly added, "I had hoped to pick some of those seeds that taste like nuts, that you find on top of the Big Ajo Mountains, but the storm . . ."

Time to go. With few words, the Papago couple plunged into the chill black night, their boys bounding around them like woolly pups.

A week went by. At the trading post, party preparations proceeded under clearing skies. The musicians. The singers. Chili con carne. Tamales steaming in cornhusk covers. Santa suit. Towering stacks of mesquite for the bonfires. At sundown Quee-Wich-Choo (Under Tree) played his antique flute and beat a hide drum. His brother danced, copper conchos and bells at his belt, rattles from knee to ankle. As the part-pagan, part-Christian celebration began, two boys darted across the clearing to Mrs. Kater.

Mrs. Kater lifted the lid of a yucca basket. Inside were eight seeds, which taste like nuts, from the top of Big Ajo Mountains. The gesture filled Mrs.

Man's church in nature's cathedral, the Chapel of the Holy Cross at Sedona is set in the red rock country of Oak Creek Canyon.

Kater's mind. She thought of the two tiny figures climbing faint trails along perilous cliffs higher and higher through the gale and ice to the crags where the seeds are found.

"It is the loveliest Christmas present I have ever had," she told the boys. And then it was Mrs. Kater's turn to weep, in humility and joy.

Charlie Cough was born in the Month of the Ripening Melon, in the year that the white man's post office opened near his home on the Gila River. One hundred years later he died, in a suburb of a metropolis of a million. He was grandson to Mo-liee, chief interpreter between his Maricopa tribe and the Mexicans before the Gadsden Purchase. Charlie, like his father, Pete, had no last name until a white soldier took notice of his habit of clearing his throat before speaking.

A branch of Yuman Indians, the Maricopas broke with the main tribe and struck an alliance with the Pimas in exchange for farms. As a male of an important family, Charlie as a boy was schooled in timeless lore. He learned to converse fluently in nine languages. Medicine men revealed the import of dreams and the power of songs and dances. Even as civilization surged up against his cotton fields and pastures, Charlie Cough preferred his meals of mashed mesquite beans and corn *pinole*. The family of Charlie and his wife, Susie, multiplied, and many of their sons and grandsons fought overseas wars, and joined the white man's churches. Charlie did not rebuke them, but he lectured them indirectly:

"To help another person is the way of the good man. To be partner with nature is the path of goodness. There is no room in the good heart and soul for greed. Truth is in the cycle of four. Observe, there are four seasons and four directions: the wind of strength from the north, the light of new life from the east, the peace of day's end of the west, and the healing warmth of the south. So, too, the dances are in sets of four, through the night until dawn, the moment of rebirth."

When Charlie felt the last of his strength ebbing, he requested an Indian burial. He would be pleased if the Christian choir would sing, and the preacher might read from the Book, but he also yearned for the chants of Mo-liee and speeches of his kinsmen.

He lay dying four days and four nights. His relatives assembled from throughout the Southwest. During the ordeal they told and retold complimentary Charlie Cough stories, within his hearing, to comfort him. He died in early evening. At dawn the Christian service was followed by Maricopa chants. Charlie Cough's body was cremated on a sacramental mesquite pyre,

114

and his ashes buried in a grave dug by his son. The excavated earth, which had been grouped in four mounds symbolic of the four eternal truths, was carefully returned to the grave. The ceremony ended with a grandson recalling Charlie Cough's last advice to his people:

"Learn the new, if you must, but do not forsake the old."

Outside, the noon sun baked the treeless earthen plaza and *Yaponcha*, the wind god, clawed at the chinked stone battlements. Inside, cool serenity. Whitewashed plaster walls. Simple furniture. Circle of friends. Old man talking.

"It is my seventy-eighth year," he said. "I no longer go for the salt as I did when young—fourteen days into the Grand Canyon to load my pack too heavy for any other man to carry. All that work! But I still run to my fields of squash and corn."

His voice sadly browsed his attic of hard memories. His children were all dead of foreign scourges, and anguish still lumped his throat when he passed their graves. He scorned exile schools, meddling social workers, modern society. His birthright was Hopi. . . .

To need no alarm clock, in a pueblo where *Tca'akmongwi* in dawn's first glow cried communiqués of the sun priests to the people . . . to depend upon the reinforcing bonds of clans and families and sense ancestral ties (that woven yucca bowl from which the woman sifts grit from sand-parched corn has not changed in twenty centuries) . . . to dwell so harmoniously with nature that fat-kernel corn could be brought off in a growing season of one hundred thirty-three days and a moisture fall of only twelve inches of rain in a year . . . to preface each meal by pitching a pinch of corn meal heavenward and reciting, "*Tewa* (Sun), we give this to you" . . . to be of kind, sharing, gentle, friendly reputation.

At the time of your marriage, to witness the women of your clan throwing ceremonial mud at your bride-to-be (she is stealing their sweetheart!) . . . and at the time a son is born, to enjoy the naming ritual: the babe bathed in yucca soap and cedar water, and each of the mother's womenfolk presenting the infant with a different name, signifying acceptance into the clan . . . to give only love to your children, so that they grow up without guilt and rebellion (by leaving the discipline and punishment to the uncles).

To become familiar with a host of two hundred fifty Kachina gods with specific functions within the mystical realm of *Massau'u*, the Great Spirit. And in time of danger and crisis, to go beseeching among deities of other worlds . . . to believe that following a period of earthquake, polluted water, and fouled air, there will come a Day of Purification, when all men are equal and united

Nearest to Phoenix of the man-made reservoirs along the Salt River, Saguaro Lake churns with all manner of water sports on weekends, but weekday evenings can be as peaceful as the South Pacific.

. . . to be convinced that the Hopi once progressed through a hell of greed, warfare, hatred, and violence, and must never pay that price again.

"Our women must carry our water from the valleys to the top of this mesa," said the old chief. "Yet we are clean. Our cornstalks are short, but our ears are full. This day we are open to these new friendships. May I go as welcome to any house in Phoenix?

"Upon what does the white man base his hope for a better future? Six thousand years of so-called civilization interrupted by only a few hundred years of peace on earth?"

The late Kate Crozier had had the last laugh on many a friend and enemy, red and white, which was one of the comforts of age 120.

Crozier was living with his son, Roy, a mile from Peach Springs on the Hualapai Indian Reservation south of Grand Canyon.

"You sit here," said Roy to a visitor, indicating a chair facing Kate, who sat on an army bunk. They are the Pine Tree People, fewer than seven hundred. In the old days they hunted game and wild food and traded buckskins for Hopi corn and Navajo blankets. They were given land deemed unsuited for white needs.

"I've heard Mr. Crozier was an Indian scout."

Roy addressed his father at length in the Hualapai tongue. As the old man listened he made a stirring picture. His gray hair hung to his shoulders, and it was gathered in a blue bandana. His brows were black. A white mustache framed a firm chin. Blind, he wore dark glasses. He answered his son in Hualapai.

"My father," Roy translated, "says he was a scout for General Crook. He enlisted as a private in 1882, and he once helped chase Geronimo into Mexico."

Another question in English. Many minutes of Hualapai.

Then Roy said, "He saw three of Geronimo's band hanged. Since he left

the Army, he has worked with the white man as prospector and cowboy. He has been an Indian policeman and a member of the tribal council, and now he is a cattleman. He is a full-blooded Hualapai, born near here." Kate also recalled the Ghost Dance of 1889, when the people were so desperate under white rule, they danced for months in the belief that slain warriors could be restored to life. That was the year a Kingman newspaper recommended that Hualapai rations "be mixed with a plentiful supply of arsenic." Kate smiled faintly and grasped his cane. Much Hualapai. Roy said in English:

"My father is one who fought the railroad and worked to establish our reservation. For this he was given a herd of cattle by his people. He believes that his blindness was caused by brush hitting him in the face as he rode after stock."

A man of so many years must have many relatives?

Kate turned to Roy. Roy translated. The old man lifted his hand as he spoke for a long time. Roy said, "He has but one son and two daughters, but he can count twenty grandchildren. They are so many, and they live from Los Angeles to Oklahoma."

And how does he spend his day? More Hualapai. "He used to get around by himself," said Roy, "even after he went blind in 1922. But in the last few years he has had to rest in bed, and it is not often he can go by himself to the store or cafe. He says he is growing weaker all over."

To this moment, Kate Crozier had not spoken one word of English. The visitor grasped his hand for a farewell shake.

"Listen, buddy," said Kate. "It's nice having people like you drop in for a visit. I'm getting old, and nobody pays much attention to an old Indian. Well, so long, pal."

CHAPTER SEVEN

Canyon and River

In 1883 the first tourists to arrive at Grand Canyon were informed by pioneer guide John Hance that he had dug it with a shovel and piled up the dirt to form San Francisco Peaks. In 1902 a steam-powered Toledo automobile reached Grand Canyon, practically hand-carried by the driver and three passengers across seventy-five miles in five days. In 1927 what appeared to be a gigantic centipede slithered down Kaibab Trail: forty-eight men packing a 548-foot-long steel cable for a suspension bridge. In 1955 Bill Beer and John Daggett swam the Colorado River through Grand Canyon, rapids and all, wearing water wings. In 1966 Tommy Manis, age ten, accelerated down Hopi Point and sailed his bicycle off the South Rim—and lived to tell about it. In 1970 William Moyes, an Australian, flew a glider-kite to the bottom of Grand Canyon and was fined $150 "for holding a special event in a national park without a permit." In 1971 John Boggess, wanting to quit as cook at Phantom Ranch at the bottom of the Grand Canyon, was sixteen pounds overweight for a mule ride. Boggess solved his dilemma by calling in a helicopter.

To me, the Grand Canyon of Arizona is *first*, a mirror of human nature, and *second*, an awesome phantasmagory. This notion waves a red flag at customary Canyon concepts, as expressed by Dr. Joseph Wood Krutch: "The most revealing single page of earth's history open on the face of the globe." Or by naturalist John Burroughs: "The world's most wonderful spectacle, ever changing, alive with a million moods." Or by Senator Henry F. Ashurst: "No prose poet has ever dipped pen deep enough into the ink of temerity to attempt a complete description." Or by historian J. Donald Hughes: "Man has always found the Canyon mysterious, filled with awe-inspiring power, strangely attractive and repellent, beautiful and charged with meaning." Or author Frank Waters, "Its heart is the savage, uncontrollable fury of all the inanimate universe, and at the same time the immeasurable serenity that succeeds it. It is creation."

As held by individuals, the attitudes are valid. But the record also shows that while man is transfigured by this masterpiece of erosion, he is also unmasked as a shameless braggart, a playful bumpkin, an insensitive clod, a self-deifying snob, a feckless victim, a noble creature, an intrepid explorer, and every so often, a most lucky fellow.

First impressions being so strong, I date my humanly viewpoint to a summer long ago when as a Boy Scout leader I accompanied a troop of Pima Indian tenderfeet on their first camp at the Canyon. A twelve-year-old lad leaned over the rim and listened to the distant whisper of the river. "Long way to carry water," said he, whose endless chore at home was fetching pails from a community spigot. It was ever thus; the world's superlative natural wonder reduced to manageable human terms.

Only forty-eight years after the arrival of Columbus to America, Don Garcia López de Cárdenas discovered Grand Canyon. From where the Spaniards perched on the rim they underestimated rock spires as equal to the height of the Tower of Seville. López cursed the Canyon as a cruel obstacle in his quest of the mythical Seven Cities of Cíbola.

In the next three hundred years, no more than a half dozen white parties reached the Canyon. Despite its size it offered no valleys for farming, no apparent treasures for digging, sparse beaver for trapping, and few souls for saving. Scenic value was yet to be invented. . . . "Horrid," was James O. Pattie's reaction in 1825. Army Lieutenant J. C. Ives reconnoitered the Canyon in 1857 and notified Washington, "Ours has been the first and will doubtless be the last party of whites to visit this profitless locality. It seems intended by nature that the Colorado River, along the greater portion of its lonely and majestic way, shall be forever unvisited and undisturbed."

120

The Hopi village of Moenkopi amid its age-old fields of gourds and corn.

Apache dancers, Flagstaff Pow Wow Parade.

Twining a burden basket, an Apache woman follows methods passed from mother to daughter.

Flowered meadow near Alpine in the White Mountains exhibits Arizona's diversity of climates. At eight thousand feet elevation, the meadow receives twenty inches of rain per year, and the average summer temperature range is 40–77 degrees.

Mighty Salt River Gorge is crossed by U. S. 60 midway between Globe and Show Low in eastern Arizona. The Salt—named for a flavor imparted by alkaline formations —annually yields enough water to cover seven hundred thousand acres, one foot deep.

Rumps turned to the wind, a string of cow ponies awaits a White Mountains storm.

In the breeding ground of show champions, Hereford cows and calves graze a White Mountains range.

Cut and wooded redoubts along the Apache Trail were used by mountain tribes in swift raids on the more peaceful farming peoples before the coming of the white man.

At 726 feet, the second tallest dam ever built by the Bureau of Reclamation, Hoover Dam impounds the prime attraction of Lake Mead National Recreation Area along borders of Arizona and Nevada. The dam holds enough concrete to make a two-lane road coast to coast, and the lake provides a water playground 115 miles long.

Foresight was perhaps too much to expect of a junior officer. Still, if Lieutenant Ives were reincarnated at Grand Canyon for a Labor Day weekend, one wonders what he would think of some 25,000 people crushed together in one tiny town to celebrate the Golly Gully, of a physicist measuring decibel levels exceeding those of Chicago's Loop, of irritated motorists circling, circling for a parking space in a park of a thousand square miles, of rangers taking camping reservations a year in advance, of tourists playing outrageous caricatures of themselves, including a California teen-ager dashing to the rim and calling back, "Hey, Dad, the tide's out!" And Sister complaining, "Isn't there a hamburger drive-in?" And Dad independently concocting everybody else's witticism, "Now *that's* what I call a *hell* of a hole in the ground!" And Mom asking half-seriously, "Was part of it built as a WPA project?" At Bright Angel Lodge, with his back turned to the gorge, Edward N. Westcott must have written his turgid line, "There's about as much human nature in some folks as there is in others, if not more."

Consider Major John Wesley Powell. Nearly all history books hold him to be the first man to negotiate the Colorado through the Grand. A good bet, he wasn't. Since six hundred prehistoric sites testify to Indian occupation of the Canyon surely as long ago as 4,000 years, and perhaps 12,000 years, probably the first man (or woman) to run the river was *red*. Moreover, Powell's epic 1869 expedition is haunted by a delicious, ever-so-human likelihood—that a Caucasian, James White, two years earlier was flushed down the Colorado against his will. White crawled ashore starved and blistered at Callville (now flooded by Lake Mead) on September 7, 1867. He babbled a sketchy but plausible story of being attacked by Indians in the San Juan River country and casting off on an unprovisioned raft of cottonwood poles lashed with a lariat. White's delirious accident, contributing no insight into the last unexplored void in the American West, has been resented by admirers of Powell's carefully prepared and executed scientific voyage.

The personality of Powell has suffered in his canonization. True enough, the major had his sober side. He was the nation's first great bureaucrat—father of the Bureau of Ethnology, the Geological Society, and the Bureau of Reclamation—but he wasn't a stuffed shirt. On the cathedral-quiet chasms between white-water rapids, the one-armed veteran of Shiloh would bellow out earthy ballads, such as Whittier's:

> *Old Floyd Ireson, for his hard heart,*
> *Tarred and feathered and carried in a cart*
> *By the women of Marblehead!*

The first stone was placed September 20, 1906, the last February 5, 1911, and the toil and travail between those two components of Roosevelt Dam were an Arizona epic. At last the feast-and-famine Salt River was harnessed for the benefit of an entire state's economy. Today, when Roosevelt Lake infrequently fills to capacity, floodwaters over the dam's spillways are caught by a succession of smaller dams downstream.

123

Moderns who derive deep spiritual meaning from the quieter moods of Grand Canyon are philosophical ancestors to ancient man. Four-thousand-year-old figurines found in canyon caves indicate that prehistoric peoples ascribed religious significance to the world's greatest gorge.

In the century after Powell, some thirty million people came to the Canyon, with an annual visitation now of 2.5 million. How many experienced spiritual enrichment is beyond measure, but as people will, a goodly number chased fortune, shot the river in a hundred styles, pitted their bodies against the Canyon's geometry, inflicted all manner of stupidities upon the wildlife of the area, and cracked preposterous jokes.

William W. Bass was an original. Against the best advice of the Santa Fe railroad that "nobody will make that trip to look at a hole in the ground," Bass established at the Canyon a primitive tourist shelter, truck garden, and asbestos mine. Among his early customers was Miss Ada Diefendorf, gifted graduate pianist of the Boston Conservatory. So enthralled was she of the peach trees, the donkeys, and Bass, she married the man, bore him four children whom she reared in the depths of the Canyon, where the family laundry was a day's pack to the river, a day of scrubbing in the muddy Colorado, and a third day home. Even at that, Ada Bass met her share of celebrities: Zane Grey, John Muir, Luther Burbank, Rex Beach, Henry Ford, all guided by Bass.

From earliest times the Canyon brought out the caprice, corruption, and controversy of mankind. In 1902 J. A. Walker offered to erect a huge water wheel within the Granite Gorge to generate electricity for mining and milling. A scheme to lay a railroad from Denver to San Diego through the bottom of the Canyon cost Frank M. Brown his life in the upset of a surveying boat in 1889. Next year Robert B. Stanton doggedly completed the survey, all the way to the Gulf of California.

In attempts to monopolize the fledging tourist industry in the early years of this century, questionable mining claims were exploited by Ralph Cameron. Had President Theodore Roosevelt not intervened, the Canyon today would be substantially defaced with rimside commerce and riverbank structures.

As it is, the activity on the busiest rim is concentrated at Grand Canyon Village. Within the Canyon itself only one work of man makes much of a show.

Since 1928 the Kaibab suspension bridge has provided a dry crossing for hikers and mule trains between the Canyon rims. Incredibly, in the more than six decades since the daily mule trains have stepped down Bright Angel Trail, no customer's life has been lost. Each day of mixing recalcitrant mules and nervous tourists has produced another choice anecdote: the doctor who fell out of his saddle and walked alongside his mule for the entire trip; dignified Marshal Foch of France mounted on a mule named TNT thought of the Canyon, "What a marvelous place to throw your mother-in-law"; the Russian Cosmonaut, Georgy Beregovoy, who clambered onto a Canyon mule and gravely announced to reporters, "If I perish, I left my will in my hotel room."

Treatment of wild animals by man at the Canyon has swung from ill-advised conservation to corrective control. After setting aside the North Kaibab game preserve in 1906, the government pressed a policy of predator reduction. Wolves were exterminated, lions, bobcats, and eagles removed by the hundreds, coyotes by the thousands. Relieved of natural enemies (including man), deer populations exploded to a hundred thousand, far beyond the carrying capacity of the range. By 1924 the deer were cropping their browse to ground level and chewing pine bark as high as they could reach. In desperation, the government condoned one of the oddest experiments in game management and film exposure. The Hollywood movie mogul, Jesse Lasky, paid $5,000 to an Arizona cowboy to drive ten thousand deer across the Canyon to better range, past Lasky's grinding cameras. To make the drive, in November 1924, more than a hundred Navajo Indians were hired and equipped with bells. The deer, paying no attention to the script, eluded the beaters.

We moderns smile. But we are heirs to an uglier consequence of man at Grand Canyon. Today the park is infested by thousands of wild burros, descendants of pioneer pack trains. Precious as burros are made to appear in fiction, in real life they are feisty monopolists of territory and water holes. Desert bighorn sheep decline as burros devour grass, brush, trees, and large numbers of park service signs. Attempts to round up the burros have proven as futile as the Great Deer Drive.

Curiosity about Canyon wildlife prompted another bizarre project in 1937. On the assumption that Shiva Temple, a mile-high mountain inside the Canyon, had never been climbed, an elaborate expedition was sponsored by the American Museum of Natural History. Scientists speculated that erosion had isolated Shiva as an independent biological unit—a three-hundred-acre mesa possibly stocked with strange creatures. Fired with imagination, Sunday supplements envisioned live dinosaurs and saber-toothed tigers. But no. On Shiva Temple the explorers found familiar plants and rodents, deer bones, coyote tracks, and

126

Indian artifacts. And most embarrassing of all, an empty Kodak film carton.

Exploitation of the Canyon coincided with advances in transportation. In the process, people allowed a goodly number of automobiles to slip over the rims. A man blinded by snow and fog backed off Hopi Point, only to be saved by a rock ledge. In 1952 another man neglected to set his parking brake, and his new car and all his belongings vanished over the north rim. Some months later a ranger climbed down to find the car sitting next to the hulk of a 1926 touring car. Being first in anything at the Canyon is not easy. Another shell, that of a 1967 sedan, lies a thousand feet below Lipan Point, a rusting monument to a chap who lost heavily at the tables in Las Vegas and chose the Canyon as a means of self-destruction.

One aerial misadventure is notable for its happy ending. In summer, 1944, with the country at war, domestic skies swarmed with military aircraft. On the night of June 20, a B-24's engines sputtered. Three airmen dived out of the bomb bay into the inky night and opened their parachutes. As they reached what they thought would be ground level, they saw the lights of a village. Abruptly, the lights winked out. The men continued to fall—into Grand Canyon. Against all odds the trio landed without serious injury, were sighted within three days, and were led safely to the north rim.

Perhaps because so much of the nation is citified, more and more people come to the Canyon for a personal wilderness adventure. They are a continuing source of pride and anguish for park rangers who on the one hand encourage reasonable exploration, and on the other hand, cope with inevitable trouble.

"It's a violent environment," says Dr. Harvey Buchart, hiker of twenty thousand Canyon miles. "There aren't any second chances out there." Thus, on into present times, unwise and unlucky hikers are struck down by exhaustion, heat, thirst, and flash flood. Best known of the Canyon hikers is Colin Fletcher, ex-Commando, who clambered alone from one end of the park to the other more or less following the river on the plateaus. How personally some backpackers feel about the Canyon is suggested in Fletcher's book, *The Man Who Walked Through Time:* "The difference between flying over Grand Canyon and living in it is like the difference between . . . seeing a beautiful woman . . . and making deeply satisfying love to her."

Even wilder have been the antics and encounters of that variegated breed compelled to follow Major Powell (or was it James White?) down the gut of the Grand . . . 161 nerve-rasping rapids in the 300 miles from Lee's Ferry to Lake Mead . . . the Big League of river-running. Again, the record is altogether human: tragic losses somehow redeemed by accomplishment.

Until Nathan Galloway came along, everybody ran the Grand with as much

Accessible streams such as this brook in the White Mountains are stocked with hatchery-raised trout, but at the highest headwaters survive a remnant of the Arizona native trout: small, olive of back and gold of belly, with rosy gills indicating close relationship to the cutthroat trout.

finesse as a moth diving down a bathtub drain, and often with similar results. But Galloway, a trapper, in a style borrowed from Canadian mountain men, *backed down* the Colorado's rapids stern-first, in light, flat-bottomed, compartmented cataract boats more kayak than skiff. As sports cars compared to dump trucks, the cataract boats went through in 1897, dodging the worst holes and boulders. Galloway took another party through in 1909, from Green River, Wyoming, to Needles, California, in nine weeks, without one upset. Using the Galloway method, the Kolb brothers, Ellsworth and Emery, negotiated the river in 1911 and 1912 for the first motion pictures and an ever-fresh, best-selling book, *Through the Grand Canyon,* brightened with humor and irony. The Kolbs tell how, in Cataract Canyon, they found evidence of a flood in debris twenty-five feet above normal river level. And among the smashed boats, battered toys, and sticks of furniture from faraway civilization: "A corked bottle containing a faded note, undated, requesting the finder to write to a certain lady in Delta, Colorado."

Emery is something of a natural wonder in his own right. As mule riders turn under the first switchback of Bright Angel Trail, he pops his head from his photographic studio and lectures in his thin, wavering voice, "The gentleman on the fourth mule must remove his smoked glasses!" At a recent ninetieth-birthday party he amused a large gathering with memories of developing his film in a mine tunnel and washing prints at a spring deep within the Canyon. Among his customers were three U. S. Presidents. After all the exploits, the fifty thousand canyonside lectures, the international honors, did Emery Kolb retain unfulfilled ambitions? "Yes," he sighed, "I'd like to catch one more good-looking young saloon girl."

For every triumphant Kolb, the first six decades of Canyon river-running produced a dozen victims: upsets, strandings, crashes, drownings; fragile dreams of puny men dashed by a river capable of transporting 27,000,000 tons of silt and sand past Bright Angel Point in a single day. Not until 1927 was the river run for fun. Satisfying a childhood yearning, millionaire Clyde Eddy recruited six college boys as oarsmen and took along a dog and a bear cub for laughs.

With huffs and hisses and clangs and toots, the White Mountain Scenic Railroad hauls steam-train buffs through Arizona's high country on forty-mile excursions daily during summertime. On a logging track leased from the Apache tribe, the "puffer-bellies" pause for nature studies and photography and lunch. Says Engineer Reed Hatch, "I guess the steam engine is the closest thing to being alive of any inanimate thing I know."

Somehow they made it through, with only two desertions, one lost boat, and no injuries more serious than sunburn. Next year, Big Red demanded tribute; the sweep scow of honeymooning Bessie and Glen Hyde was found empty, snagged in a backwater below ferocious Mile 232 Rapid.

As a Canyon anthropocentric, Haldane (Buzz) Holstrom is unequaled. In Coquille, Oregon, while working as a service station attendant, he obtained a cedar log, which he sawed into planks for a fifteen-foot boat. Alone, in October 1937, he cast off at Green River, and seven weeks later, he emerged at Lake Mead. He turned from fame and fortune, saying, "I find I have already had my reward, in the doing of the thing."

130

Next year the first women (white women, that is) ran the river with Norman D. Nevills. Botanists Lois Jotter and Dr. Elzada Clover lent scientific substance to the trip, and Nevills, as much a showman as oarsman, kept the world on the edge of the Canyon with rumors of disaster. Through the 1940s, Nevills with his fleet of trim plywood cataract boats was the dominant figure on the river.

There are other names, other deeds, worth remembering. River-running had become commonplace by 1954 (through the Grand that year floated 218 people) when a former submarine commander, Dock Marston, sailed the first motorboat down the Colorado. Two years later Jim Jordan and Rod Sanderson negotiated the Grand in the first *outboard* motorboat. In 1951 Jim and Bob Rigg rowed a Nevills cataract boat through in an astonishing two and a half days, nonstop. The first two Canyon trips by Georgie White, who did more to popularize river-running than anyone, were by life jacket, sans boat. In July of 1960 New Zealander John Hamilton led three Buehler jet boats *up* the Colorado's worst rapids—leaving little more to prove. The following year, when an anonymous daredevil rode a truck inner tube from Lee's Ferry to Phantom Ranch, accompanied by his toy bulldog in a Volkswagen inner tube, the world yawned. And today, ten thousand city men, grandmothers, housewives, and half-grown children take on Sockdolager, Grapevine, Upset, Hermit, Horn, and Lava, the worst white water of the Colorado, aboard improved inflated rigs pioneered by Georgie White.

"That one big hole at Lava Falls can be sixteen feet deep," says Gaylord Staveley, who continues the guide service founded by Nevills. "If you hit it head-on, think of your seat in the boat as the floor of your living room. The mass of water that is about to crash down on your head is the ceiling—of the second floor above you." Little wonder, Staveley will smoke three cigars studying a rapid he will run in three puffs. Yet despite the risks, the numbers of people willing to run the Grand seem infinite.

In 1970 park rangers reluctantly placed limits on white-water trips to control pollution and preserve some semblance of wilderness. Topside, the park service began a registration-reservation program for Canyon campgrounds. The action followed long, agonizing debates about the sociology and philosophy of an ideal park experience. Do most modern people want solitude, or companionship, in their national parks? If the park service continues to *develop* parks, will some day none remain undeveloped? If Americans accept quotas on theater tickets, must they insist on crowding into a full-house national park and sitting on someone's lap? Is the notion still valid that "the wilderness and the idea of wilderness is one of the permanent homes of the human spirit?"

Under an angler's sky, escapees from Arizona's desert heat cast for rainbows in chill Luna Lake just east of Alpine.

CHAPTER EIGHT

God's Country

Ten thousand wild iris nod beneath a bowl of cotton cloud. Down a brushy draw, dust rises from the pawing of a Hereford bull. A cow elk glides like smoke against a row of regal spruce.

Summertime. God's Country, Arizona.

An indefinite area, this. No political subdivision describes a precise perimeter or designates a center. This expanse of wooded highland embraces Apache National Forest, as big as Delaware, the equal-size Fort Apache Indian Reservation, and a goodly portion of Sitgreaves National Forest. Humanity is diffused into ranch houses and crossroad hamlets and one-street towns, many of them unincorporated. Influenced by elevation and topography, a single mountain may rise through three major climatic zones, and host a dozen different habitats: thickets of chaparral, grassy *cienegas*, turquoise lakes, timberline, spring-fed streams, upland desert.

But the people who reside along this reach of hundred miles of Mogollon Rim think of their land as a whole, and they use an informal name for it. The otherwise unsentimental cowpoke met packing salt along Hurricane Creek allows that all seems well with "God's Country." The amateur gem seeker picking ten pounds of agate from Limestone Canyon says his "braggin'" rocks are exactly what he expected in "God's Country." When Round Valley whips the visiting team 44–0, the fullback's mom presumes no less than divine assistance for "God's Country."

May that summer be remembered as The Time You Went Up Baldy. Even more, child of mine, may you go again, with your own tomboy daughter, to a Baldy unspoiled: wild and elemental and startling, from the close details of strawberries and hailstones to the tramontane vistas of marching timber and boiling nimbus.

That is how Captain George M. Wheeler, Army explorer, saw Baldy in eastern Arizona, in the 1870s: "The view from the summit was the most magnificent and effective of any among the large number that have come under my observation. . . . Outstretched before us lay the tributaries of seven principal streams . . . four main mountain peaks . . . valley lands surpassing any I have before seen. The view of the landscape to the east is the most marvelous beauty of form and color. Mountain, forest, valley, and streams are blended into one harmonious whole. . . . Few world-wide travelers in a lifetime could be treated to a more perfect landscape, a true virgin solitude, undefiled by the presence of man."

How fortunate you were that day, with Arizona's primitive lands shrinking, to find Baldy much the same. When you go again, if your memory is keen, you may recall the Greenwald cabin. Fred and Frances had a houseful: a gregarious gathering of horsemen, ranchers, hikers, foresters, biologists, and other admirers of wilderness. Surely two who will remain in your memory were Nelson Lupe, from the White Mountain Apache Tribe, and his wife, dark and handsome in her long traditional dress and patient with your endless questions about her many children.

After dinner the adults droned on in a seminar of history and geography. Scraps of intense discussion fell on your ten-year-old ears:

"Mount Baldy, rising from 9,000 to 11,590 feet, highest peak in the second highest range of Arizona." "Because of its extraordinary beauty, one of the first Primitive Areas set aside by the Forest Service, in 1932." "A mountain of frowning lava bluffs, devil's rock slides, fearless skunks, and fighting native trout." "Covered with spruce and fir, pine and aspen. Nearly forty inches of moisture (mostly snow) per year. The only Primitive Area in Arizona wholly within the spruce-fir zone. Unique for its wet grassy meadows, where lady's-slippers sink their toes into perpetual moisture. Lair of the bear and cougar,

OVERLEAF:

Friendly and inviting in summer, this great open park in the White Mountains will cradle fence-deep snow packs during winter.

Homely as cow chips, no more to look at than a stump-tied bull at fly time, kinky as a colt in high oats, born in a shack so poor a dog could crawl through the cracks, plumb weak north o' the ears, not worth a cow on the front porch—but he's a cowboy, and his compensation is drinking unpolluted snowmelt straight from the source.

135

Madonna and child, mule-deer style.

138

mink and beaver. Nesting place of the raven and eagle and turkey. Summer home of elk and deer."

But Baldy was not included in the Wilderness Preservation Act. Congress directed that primitive areas should receive further study. Congress made certain that adding any more wilderness would be a long and difficult process. First, study committees. Then, public hearings. Then, agency recommendations, followed by endorsement by the President, and even then, each wilderness would require further, separate action by Congress.

You were a party to the first stages for Baldy. Your friend Fred Greenwald was chairman of the Arizona Conservation Council's initial study committee. The droning grown-up words nearly put you to sleep, but you woke when Nelson Lupe spoke. A gigantic graying Indian, you could almost imagine him in breechcloth and moccasins, negotiating across a council fire in some fortress hardwood canyon.

"That mountain is sacred to my people. In the crevasses of Baldy, you may see the prayer beads sacrificed by the Apache. The summit lies within our reservation. We hold half the mountain. The national forest, the remainder. The mountain should be managed as a unit. So our tribe has set aside more than seven thousand acres as primitive area for five years. That is what the Indians are willing to do, while waiting to see what the white man is willing to do."

Next day, at last, you saw for yourself, lifted up Baldy by a sturdy cow pony, up from Phelps Botanical Area by Sheep Crossing Trail, up the swales of bluebells. You went ducking dangerous stobs of Douglas fir, flushing a band of does with fawns, dismounting to caress a columbine, lying down for a drink from a rivulet as clear as topaz and so cold it hurt your teeth. You chucked chunks of bark at the laggard pack mules, and at pauses we rested the horses in Baldy's rare atmosphere, and you looked back over your shoulder at the thunderheads grumbling among the foothills down below.

As if to remind you of human scale, the old mountain growled and shuddered where you stopped for lunch. Fearsome flashes of lightning stabbed the summit, while in a grove of moss-draped fir you held your shivering horse and hid under a poncho from a barrage of ice. Then, how warming was the bonfire, and how restoring was that coffee brewed in a tin can by a forest supervisor.

At Baldy's dome, bare and windswept, you overheard a scrap of dissent, "Why should there be wilderness where only people who are rich and healthy and in the prime of their lives, may go?" And quite correctly you blurted, "Well, I'm not rich, and I'm not strong, but I can make it, and we've got a lot of old folks with us today, don't we?" As well as anyone, you defended the cause—

Wilderness is the residual soul of America's original resource. It is scrubbed air and undammed streams and a patch of monkey flower. It is contradiction of mortality and timelessness, upon which man may ponder. But where roads go, where engines roar, where untested hordes may crowd and deface—is not wilderness. Where the logging roads extend, inviting blitzkrieg hunters and caravan campers—is not wilderness. Wilderness is ". . . beyond civilization . . . where the earth and its community of life are untrammeled by man, where man himself is a visitor who does not remain."

May you go again to Baldy, and the child of your child, to taste a handful of tart crimson strawberries mixed with ice freshly fallen from the sky.

A wife in hair curlers blows a kiss. A sleepy child waves listlessly. Thirty dogs signal the passage of the horsemen through Clifton at five o'clock in the morning. The first annual Coronado Trail Ride is on the move.

Along Chase Canyon the horses labor, through the sterile chute of rock inclined upward for ten miles into folded horizons where eighty years before Plymouth Rock, the Conquistadors found "a worse way than ever." The animals plod past tunnels of abandoned railroads, under the drifting heaps of over-burden expelled from the Morenci mine pit, through foundations sagging like gravestones for the ghost town, Metcalf. The mounts wend up ridges under Grey's and Mitchell peaks, and press across ranges of wheat grass and brush to Eagle Creek. Thirty-two miles. Feeling every furlong, the men wash dust from their throats, down supper, crawl into bedrolls, and die.

They make an odd collection of corpses. A small-town banker with a yen for fly fishing. A country doctor with no chance to revel at home. A trial judge fleeing pleas and sentences. A rodeo roper turned cattle inspector. A jeweler and a lumberman and a grocer. And a few guests from the big city. Their all-too-brief purgatory is contrived of moans and snores, aching joints and smarting blisters, recollections of yesterday and premonitions of tomorrow.

Resurrection begins at 4 A.M., when cook and swamper bang last night's grounds from the enameled pot, toss an armload of applewood onto last night's coals, and rustle breakfast. At first light a city dude tentatively throws a tender thigh over a lean, sinewy sixteen-year-old gray stallion named Champagne, of a strain favored by stockmen along the Coronado Trail. "He'll draw up like a gutted snowbird," the owner has warned, "but he'll go all day."

Breaking camp, the riders follow a gravel road fording Eagle Creek at a dozen places, through patented homesteads wooded with sycamore and maple. The real estate boom has not reached the Eagle. Yet. No garish signboards tout platted paradises; the transition zone retains its power of understatement:

140

"Unknown" read many of the headstones in the cemetery of Old Fort Apache near Whiteriver in the White Mountains. Founded in 1870 and not abandoned until 1922, the fort is one of the few army camps of the West ever besieged by Indians. Extant today are horse barns, officer's quarters, commandant's house, and other original structures.

Arms locked on horns, boots set to put on the brakes, a professional bulldogger plies his trade at Scottsdale's Parada del Sol rodeo.

close-cropped grama grass, gray-green pinyon, huddles of ponderosa seedlings. By midmorning the string of irregular cavalry passes Honeymoon Cabin, marking the start of a cruel climb that quickly lathers the horses. The day turns hot. Welcome breaks are taken at historic Four Drag Cabin, built of adz-squared logs, and at a rancher's roundup shack at the head of Squirrel Canyon. Here the riders pause for a lunch of beer and beef, from the pack of Hercules, the mule. Already, some of the *caballeros* are bone-weary. Champagne's rider has pulled on a pair of long johns as a desperate defense against a four-cornered trot. He groans when the leader, an ex-cowboy, calls boots and saddles.

The narrow trail, prehistoric in origin, rises through pines that were mature when Bull Run crackled, were juvenile when Concord flamed. Squirrel Creek is choked with watercress, and its banks are lush with spicy fern. Snags often block the trail, more so than in the early times when the horse trails were the highways of the Coronado country. Back then, every cantankerous mossy-horn steer had to be choused from his thicketed draw, but today's tame cattle mostly gather themselves, and the trails are used but seldom, for doctoring, for packing salt, for mending fence.

Up, up, the trail snakes. Pine gives way to spruce; walnut to violets and skunk cabbage; oak to buttercups. Somewhere between seven and eight thousand feet are sighted the vibrant, verdant healers of Arizona's high forests, the quaking aspens. "Quaky country," says a rider of the blanched trunks and pea-green foliage trembling in the softest breath. Now the horses are halted at every switchback to gasp in the high thin air.

The plan was to ride directly from the crest of the Mogollon Rim to Reno Lookout at nine thousand feet, thence down Conklin Ridge to a camp, pitched in advance by the cook, on Reservation Creek. But the verve of the riders exceeds the numbness of their backsides.

"I recall as a boy getting around through Bear Wallow in no more than a couple of hours."

Along this section of Blue River in eastern Arizona, in 1540, Coronado and his men likely passed in their search for the Seven Cities of Cíbola. The expedition got as far as Kansas.

Huzzah! votes the group. At first the slope down Bear Wallow is gentle, through waterlogged loam where the horses sink past their fetlocks. A convention of deer adjourns ahead. Underfoot wapiti sign fertilizes dandelions. Felled groves of aspen silently indict a beaver reclamation project; a hen turkey bustles off with her flock of hand-size poults. Twenty-five miles from breakfast, the world is still touched with beauty.

Now the canyon turns inside out. Crisscrossing its steep and boulder-strewn bottom, the trail is filled by slides that chute down near-vertical cliffs. Dudes and natives alike loosen their toes in their stirrups, ready if need be to leap free. A horse might survive such a tumble; a man likely not.

The truth is revealed. Townsmen of any age cannot travel as fast as cowboys could, when they were boys. Neither can old cowboys. The trail tumbles down Bear Wallow seven miles, losing at least three thousand feet. Champagne's rider wonders if he can endure much more of the punishing downhill jolting. He thinks he might collapse off Champagne and that the Coronado men might kick together a cairn and leave him otherwise unmarked in a foreign forest.

One of the elderly cowboys switches his mule to the head of the column, studies blazes, and orders a right turn up a draw toward Gobbler Point. The horses are gaunt; the men, sagging. And Gobbler Point is higher than eight thousand feet. The horses steam in the afternoon chill, laboring up to panoramas of blue ridge and green meadow. For a moment, where the trail again bends over a rim, saddle aches are forgotten.

Alas, at sundown, the column loses interval, and half the riders choose a wrong turn to Reno Lookout. An hour is lost in rounding up strays. In deepening gloom the motley cortege begins its bone-rattling descent of Conklin Ridge. Camp is seven miles by eagle wing. By horse, it is eleven.

The night wears on. Eight o'clock. The men bellow at Hercules, the mule, to keep his place in line. Nine o'clock. In faint starlight the horses jump blown-down trees. Ten o'clock. Slope becomes cliff. Eleven o'clock. Shod hoofs strike sparks fighting for purchase in fractured granite. A flashlight stabs through the black ribs of a copse of pin oaks. At the brink of disaster, the leader has his comrades dismount and walk their horses to a flattish pocket of ground.

"Sorry, boys, but we'll have to bed down here, in a dry camp, with what we've got."

The thirsting horses are unsaddled and hobbled out into thin grass. Around a smoky fire talk is of food, spring water, snake medicine, and bedrolls waiting at Reservation Creek. Hercules' pack is raided. It gives up one doubtful sandwich and three cans of skunky beer. Some of the men rest on saddles and vainly try to sleep under the moist, gamy horse blankets.

"Eighteen hours we rode today," says our banker, "and we're not fighting a war or founding an empire, but supposedly taking vacations. And you know something? I'm having the time of my life."

At five o'clock in the morning the fire is buried and the riders line off Conklin Ridge. In a half hour they are approaching camp. The horse wrangler is running toward them, swinging grain sacks, grinning like a jackass with a mouthful of cactus.

"They's fresh coffee," he says. Then, "Any you boys gonna want to go a-riding after breakfast?"

Dusk. Late spring. We've been gone all day, for no better reason than to visit Pacheto Falls, framed by firs and veiled in vapor. The expedition looped through another twenty miles of Indian reservation and in all that travel, just two other humans were met: a pair of young Apache cowpunchers with straw sombreros and bony horses. The day has staged vignettes: a coyote pup awkwardly bounding after a monarch butterfly, a twenty-inch rainbow trout cleaving a riffle where no wheel has ever turned, a perfect pair of crystal doorknobs found in the ruins of a pioneer's cabin, a family of Abert's squirrels practicing high-wire stunts in a big top pine. Now we take the last leg to camp and are met by a down-canyon breeze bearing the ambrosia of fruit and vanilla.

"Bless me, Jesse, I'll bet Johnny has gone and built a peach cobbler." Yes, he has. Hastily the men turn in their mounts to a sawlog corral. They grain and rub the horses, then fetch their bottles and beers and congregate at a conversation fire near Johnny's smaller cookfire.

In town, the noise of a cocktail party begins at a bearable decibel level and rapidly rises competitively inside a closed chamber until people shout to be heard. At twilight in the wilderness, conversation is muted by the acoustics

146

"The sun shines on Brewery Gulch 330 days in the year, but there's moonshine every night," is the motto of **The Gazette** *of Bisbee. But in truth, Brewery Gulch is tame compared to its past.*

of infinity, and between preposterous tales and terrible jokes, even the cackle-and-coo of a burrowing owl filters in from beyond firelight.

Arms floured halfway to his elbows, Johnny Cosper accepts a beer for drinking while he "rassles the pots and pans." Unlike many old-time cowboys turned to vinegar, Johnny doesn't resent the loquacity of this random gather of outdoorsmen. He also refuses to change his own old-fashioned ways. He grins at "the windies," but he will not join in unless coaxed. He has hired on to cook for this town bunch strictly on his own terms—turn-of-the-century-roundup style.

"Hey, John," says a chap from Phoenix, "television had a documentary on real-life cowboys the other night. David Brinkley in New York said that cowboys are the worst-fed workers in the world. What do you think of that?" Johnny's expression of mock insult is enhanced by smoke-stimulated tears coursing through the wrinkles and white stubble of his eighty-year face.

"I never knowed a cowboy to stop eatin' long enough to complain."

Laughter. Sip of beer. Owl hoot. Johnny returns to rustling chuck, a quizzical mix of impeccable courtesy and you-be-damned integrity, painful self-reliance and fanatical faith in the work ethic. He was up two hours before the sun today, and he will not allow himself to sleep before midnight, out of eight decades of habit. He rode this country when it was stocked with lanky, slab-sided, dagger-horned Texas beeves, and when mountain man Ben Lilly was killing grizzly bears *mano a mano* and treeing fifty cougars a year along the Blue. Barbed wire, tame cattle, pickup trucks, horse trailers, branding chutes, windmills, and serums have extracted much of the risk and effort from ranching, but cattle still must be tended, herded, branded, and treated, and Johnny Cosper elects to stay active in a craft that has never organized for collective bargaining for shorter hours and better pay. Reed-thin, withdrawn into his cocoon of self-esteem, Johnny is the last of an extraordinary breed which evolved in the few generations of the one truly American experience: going West. As he clangs among his pothooks and oven lids, in pride, Johnny brings to mind that old cow camp saying, "If you think all men are equal, you ain't never been afoot and met a man ridin' a good horse."

Without doubt, range fare violates every modern dietary concept. Grease and starch are prominent. What won't fry is boiled, and what won't boil is baked, invariably well done. Anything fresher than raisins is considered rabbit food. But also undisputed, cowboys seem to thrive on the kind of food Johnny cooks. As proof of satisfaction, in a town cafe a cowboy usually will order a steak, fried, extra well.

In a calling turned around by refrigeration and dehydration, Johnny needs

148

only basics. Provide him with a quarter of beef (ours now hangs chilling on a lariat from a treefork), staples, two Dutch ovens and two pots, and he manufactures meals of great variety. His beans take all day. He culls the rocks from a sack of Colorado pintos and adds them to warm water in an oven. As the water comes to a boil, he drops in cubes of salt pork. Throughout the day the oven moves in and out of the fire, ever on the verge of a boil, taking on water from a separate pan also heating near the fire. To add cold water, insists John, would toughen the beans. In the last hour, he dices an onion and salts to taste and stirs in a palm of Eagle-brand chili powder, "long on flavor, short on heat."

Beef supplements cowboy beans. Steaks are cut about as thick as a mule's lip, floured and salted, and dropped kerplunk into smoking hot tallow. Johnny's pot roast could be set before royalty. Somehow the smoke of oak seeps through the iron oven. A cowboy cook is judged more by his bread than anything else, and Johnny is a master baker. Critical is the fussing with the coals on and under the oven. By magic Johnny knows when the center biscuit is the color of copper. Yesterday Johnny served fried chicken and rice pudding, and tomorrow it will be baked trout and cinnamon-fruit. But tonight it is beefsteak, beans, biscuits, gravy, and peach cobbler, washed down with coffee that could float a horseshoe. Johnny lifts the lid of his baking oven, flicks up the center biscuit with a gnarled forefinger, and signals the stampede with the threat, "Come and git it 'fore I throw it in the fire."

While the men wordlessly wolf down the supper, Johnny Cosper sits back a ways on his haunches and nurses his beer. When he learned to cowboy, the cook was last to eat, so as to insure that there would be enough "for the workin' hands." Now, even for this string of no-account dudes with double rations, he can no more change his custom than that owl out there, cooing and cackling.

"Autumn is a second spring when every leaf is a flower." Could Albert Camus have been, spiritually at least, in the White Mountains of Arizona in October?

Autumn is when the flatland foreigners retreat to their *ersatz* worlds. Their boisterous offspring are put away in institutions. Gone are their aluminum camps and motorbikes and transoceanic radios. A mile or more high, nature gets a creaky feeling in her bones. A sober, reflective, preparatory mood permeates the uplands. Life is weighed between the wasteful abundance of summer and the spartan larder of winter.

Roundup herds bawl down the draws, and flocks of sheep flee the rims toward warmer pastures. Big Max pumpkins shine under bleached cornstalks at Heber, and *jalapeño* peppers ripen amid the spent squash vines at Nutrioso.

149

Weaver's Needle, legendary prominence within sight of the Lost Dutchman Gold Mine, could be named for its resemblance to a shuttle, or for the mountain man Pauline Weaver.

150

With cedar smoke tanging the crisp dawns, stacks of cordwood grow by the lodges at Beaverhead.

One morning all is green; next morn, the sumac is turned cardinal, and the elder, flaxen. More hardwoods join with browns and oranges until the spectrum is complete. Aspen, reduced to shocked whispering, unloose the golden treasures hoarded for half a year, only to see the bonanzas squandered by mischievous winds and waters. Forgotten stands of oaks smear entire slopes with russet and rose.

Wildlife adjusts as the planet itself seems to turn more deliberately. The fat times are past. A trying passage lies ahead. For more needs, are fewer minutes. The jay steals from the squirrel, the nuthatch from the jay. Buck deer joust; coyotes instruct eager adolescents; migrant robins and bluebirds and flycatchers itch for a winter in Mexico.

Autumn in the White Mountains is when insects are annihilated, almost. The beetles and hoppers and flies scythed down by the northwester will not return next year, but rhinoceros beetles will reappear under porch lights and nymphs will hatch in rivulets and dragonflies will deftly maneuver the midday thermals.

Mountain autumn's Indian summer is a mild, dry lull between the violent gulf monsoons and the soaking Pacific storms. Frosty mornings. Sunny noons. Extra-blanket nights, hung with stars just beyond reach of the ponderosa boles. The dwellers of this province, close to the nuances of nature, note the signals of fall. They react in admirable ways; tend to be more honestly openhanded; turn from hustling the stranger to helping a neighbor. People need people, as longer shadows engulf the valleys that so recently were wilderness. A younger man appears with wedges and sledgehammer at an elder neighbor's house and insists on splitting the firewood because, "I sure need the exercise."

Human perspective fades in the promise of spring and the reward of summer. But for those who live in the mountains where winters can be severe, autumn is a pause for introspection. Possibly in the White Mountains of Arizona, between first frost and first snowfall, live the greatest percentage per capita of Americans who care not that the dollar buys fewer yen, that neckties narrow or widen, or that doomsayers disagree only on the time and way that the world will come to an end. It's time to core an apple from your own tree and think an eternal thought in God's Country.

What it means and how it got its name are subjects of historical debate, but the people of Patagonia in Santa Cruz County are no less proud. They've restored the town's abandoned train depot as a Western museum.

152

CHAPTER NINE

Oblique Places, Unique Names

Buzzard Roost Canyon, Wagon Tire Flat. Sockdolager Rapids, Uncle Sam Hill. Chocolate Mountain, Bottomless Pits. Hardscrabble Mesa, Cremation Creek. Big Sandy River, Newspaper Rock.

Arizona is labeled with the most colorful, most imaginative geographic terminology in the world. The boast made, let the burden of disproof rest with regions where there are not towns called Bumble Bee, no mines named Total Wreck, no creeks named Quien Sabe?, no peaks named Squaw Tit, no forts named Misery, no canyons named Wickytywiz, and no ghost towns named Copperopolis.

Let other provinces display a more unusual name than Show Low. Two Arizona pioneers dissolved their partnership in a game of seven-up. With a townsite as stakes, Marion Clark announced, "Show low, you win." Corydon Cooley responded, "Show low it is," and the turn of a card won—and named—a community.

And to this day (the residents believe), resulting in part from its novel

Modern-day name-dropper is Bernie Maher, long-time guide among the geological formations of Monument Valley. "I recall," says Maher of his thousand-foot-high monuments, "when they were just babies a few feet high!"

baptism, Show Low's soul remains that of a go-for-broke saddle-blanket gambler—an informal, speculative mountain resort ready to risk a smile on a stranger, eager to bet a diner he can't devour a seventy-two-ounce steak at one sitting (free if he can), and compelled to offer roadside chances on everything from fishin' worms to cabinsites. Of a recent year, the biggest ranch in the area was broken up and sold to neighbors who drew lots from a sombrero. That's Show Low. You can bet on it. And across the variegated face of Arizona are numerous other places of exceptional nomenclature, where the people are convinced they are set apart by their place names. The attitudes may be valid. It's difficult to imagine rollicking, adventive Show Low functioning as *Cooleyburg.*

Before the card game Show Low owned an Indian name, of course. All places of consequence did. But out of possessiveness or vanity or ignorance, the newcomers (mainly uncouth males) named nearly all of them over again. Sometimes indelicate, often lyrical, generally useful were the designations of Spaniard, Mexican, trapper, explorer, soldier, railroader, cowman, prospector, packer, and farmer. They dubbed the rivers and water holes, then the mountains and passes, and later the stage and train stops, the outposts and battlegrounds, the mines and crossroads, the steamboat landings and county seats. Name-droppers drew inspiration from Arizona's exposed geology, its ironic beauty, its intimidating scale.

Spud Rock, Pick-em-up, Government Hill. Tintown, Tonto Rim, Silver King Mine. Silent, Santa Claus, Scatterville. Wolfhole, Dead Boy Point, and Valentine.

The uninhibited catalogue endures where pioneers tasted: Salt River, Alum Gulch, Bitter Springs, Sweetwater. Where they listened: Thunder River, Roaring Springs. Where they looked: Black River, Painted Desert, Vermillion Cliffs. Where they felt: Freeze Out Canyon, Breezy Point, Agua Caliente. Where they smelled: Coffee Creek, Columbine Falls, Mint Valley, Rosebud Flat. Where they loved: Benny and Rosey creeks, lying side by side.

A strata remindful of a musical staff became Music Mountain. A hole in Navajo sandstone, Window Rock. An aperture in a lofty granite peak, Eagle Eye. Where rocks resemble Mexican cakes, Tortilla Flat. The bare dome of the state's second highest range, Mount Baldy. A deep canyon, the Devil's Windpipe.

The town of Bisbee today lurches down Mule Pass, staggers around sixty curves of Tombstone Canyon, bumps against Castle Rock, and arrives dry and disheveled at Brewery Gulch, just in time for a drink. The watering holes are not so numerous as in the days when hard-rock Slavs and Mexicans cut the coppery dust from their throats in the Hermitage, the Bonanza, the Old Crow, the Silver King, not to mention forty other saloons of frontier Bisbee. Little wonder, "The world was created for men to labor in six days a week; Brewery Gulch was created for them to roister in seven nights." Those were the days when Cockeyed Jimmy supervised the panguingui game upstairs, and a beered-up black bear slept in a tree—that is, until one night it fell and inspired an enduring Brewery Gulch axiom: "If you get drunk, don't go to sleep in a tree, at least not with a chain around your neck." During Prohibition the Hermitage was converted into a soda fountain, but in recent years the malt-stained old tavern regained a measure of respectability as headquarters of the *Brewery Gulch Gazette*, a weekly tabloid steeped in the traditions of "the West's wickedest side street."

Black Jack Canyon, Holy Joe Peak. Sandy Bob Canyon, Charlie Day Spring. Big Lue Canyon, Tom Mix Wash. French Joe Canyon, Greasy Toms Creek.

If a swarthy bartender took up a homestead in anticipation of a railroad—Black Bill Park. If a husky prospector sought his fortune in a side canyon—Big Johnny Gulch. If James Samuel Haught ran cattle on a prominence—Jim Sam Butte.

Eden and Enterprise were named by Mormon settlers seeking Utopia. Paradise and Honeymoon were first homes of newlyweds. Hope rose, briefly, in the bosoms of merchants moving to a road short cut. Through Pleasant Valley flared Arizona's bloodiest range war. Once a town named Plenty boasted of a post office with hundreds of patrons, but now Plenty is nothing.

Kim, name of a Yuma County railroad siding, began as a joke. A Southern Pacific president officially named the siding for his Chinese cook, and one day when the president's private car passed through, Kim the cook was dropped off to survey his namesake—nothing but a set of rails surrounded by desert. A following train picked up Kim, and the conductor asked him what he thought of his town.

"Fine, fine," said Kim. "Lots of room to grow!"

156

Snowflake, in a shallow swale of Silver Creek north of the Mogollon Rim, honors its founders, Snow and Flake. Fredonia, in Arizona, south of Kanab, Utah, by legend is a corruption of "free" and "doña," Spanish for "lady," or "mistress." In early days when authorities raided polygamous Mormon families residing at Kanab, the "extra wives" were spirited off to temporary quarters at Fredonia.

Single Standard Gulch, Twin Buttes, Third Mesa, Four Peaks, Fivemile Lake, Seven Mile Hill, Thirteen Mile Rock, Twenty-four Draw, Ninety-mile Desert, Thousand Wells, Million Dollar Stope.

Desperation and danger prompted Grief Hill, Fools Hollow, Doubtful Pass, Upset Rapid, Wrong Mountain, Cemetery Ridge, Lousy Gulch, Mistake Peak, The Boneyard, Graveyard Canyon, and Fort Defiance. For years after an ambush by Arizona outlaws, the bones of Mexican *vaqueros* bleached on the floor of Skeleton Canyon. Dead Man's Flat recalls a prospector who impulsively shot his stubborn horse . . . then overcome with remorse, sat down on the carcass and shot himself. Deadly happenings also gave rise to Bloody Basin, Skull Valley, and Cañon del Muerto. But Arizona's best-known morbid landmark is something of a testimony of Man Victorious. "You'll find nothing but your tombstone," a doubter cautioned Ed Schieffelin, and when Ed struck it rich, he named his mine Tombstone.

Tombstone boomed and busted on silver and revived on tourism. Among synthetic tourist attractions exist some authentic restorations, such as the Courthouse, now a state park, stage for many a territorial trial and execution. The Crystal Palace, an opulent casino with badmen bullet holes in its iron ceiling, still operates as a saloon. The Bird Cage Theatre, of late a musty museum, didn't close its doors, day or night, for three years through Tombstone's naughtiest times. The Rose Tree Inn shelters the planet's largest rose tree and countless curios. The Episcopal church, handsome frontier Gothic, is the oldest-standing Protestant church in the state. As entered into the National Register of Historic Places, St. Paul's ranks of higher historic stature than the OK Corral, Boot Hill, and the Can Can Restaurant.

Kuchaptuvela. Baboquivari. Chubwichalobi. Komoktetuvavosit. Hassayampa. Yumtheska. Lululongturqui.

By good fortune, a treasure of Indian names is left to identify geographic features. For imagery, the native namemaker was unexcelled.

The only dependable water in a sixty-mile radius in early times, Pipe Spring (now a national monument) took its name from the marksmanship of Jacob Hamblin who, in 1858 on a bet, shot the bottom out of a clay pipe without touching the sides of the bowl.

Bylas (village) – Apache, "One who does all the talking."
Arivaipa (canyon) – Pima, "Men who have committed a girlish act."
Chukut Kuk (village) – Papago, "Owl hoots."
Pan Tak (village) – Papago, "Coyote sits."
Harquahala (mountains) – Mohave, "There is water up high."
Mishongnovi (village) – Hopi, "The other of two sandstone columns remains standing."
Naahtee (canyon) – Navajo, "Toadstool causes blindness."
Awatobi (village) – Hopi, "High home of the bow people."
Parrissawampits (spring) – Paiute, "Boiling water."
Babocomari (land grant) – Papago, "Clay hanging in cell-like formations."
Lukachukai (village) – Navajo, "White patch of reeds extends out of the pass."
Topawa (village) – Papago, "It is a bean."
Chediski (mountain) – Apache, "White mountain that sits back alone."

Chuck Box Lake, Jerked Beef Butte, Red Horse Wash, Burro Creek, Cinch Hook Butte, Rawhide Mountain, Wild Bunch Pocket, Stray Horse Canyon.

Cowboys supplied their share of evocative names. Their lingo lies on storied ranges: Bronco, Haystack, Jump-Off, Jump Up, Maverick. At Pool Knoll, ranchers combined their resources for roundups. Cowboys whiled away entire winters on Poker Mountain. Where cattle roamed free, long-roping outlaws lurked. Rustler Park grew tall grass for fattening stolen stock, and Horse Thief Basin provided an easy-to-defend way station on a smuggler route once extending from Colorado to Mexico. During that period the basin's two most influential citizens were nicknamed Horse Thief Davis and Horse Thief Thompson.

Tiny open-ended towns with genuine cow-country character still interrupt Arizona's open spaces. Patagonia, with a horse museum with three Remingtons

No fewer than a dozen prominences of Arizona are named Squaw—peak or mountain. This one is in the Phoenix Mountains north of the city.

160

and weekend jackpot roping contests. Mammoth, one false-front main street winding under windmills. Young, which went eighty-five years without electricity.

Bat Canyon, Grasshopper, Dromedary Peak. Gobbler Point, Raven Butte, Wet Beaver Creek. Camelback, Partridge Wash, Turtle Back Mountain. Eagle Rock, Jackrabbit Flat, Rattlesnake Basin.

Dinosaur Canyon in Coconino County preserves the three-million-year-old tracks of gigantic reptiles. The Alligator is a low spiny ridge in Grand Canyon. North of Bumble Bee trickles Big Bug Creek, where the honored beetles still buzz. And in a saddle below Lady Bug Peak, organic farmers scoop up buckets of ladybirds to release in their aphid-infested fields.

One version of the naming of the Vulture Mine in 1863 has Henry Wickenburg hefting a rock to toss at a pesky buzzard, only to stop in his windup as he realized the stone was unusually heavy. An assay confirmed one of Arizona's richest gold strikes, which financed the Civil War and conceived Wickenburg, not so much a town as a never-ending jubilee. In and around the "Dude Ranch Capitol of the World," vacationing corporation executives allow themselves to be bossed around by fifty-dollar-a-week wranglers. The Caballeros trail ride suffers along with barbecue dinners catered in from Texas and mobile men's rooms equipped with hot-water showers. Lloyds of London insures the Jail Tree, to which outlaws were handcuffed in early times. The annual sports sensation is a miners' Olympics: a mucking contest to determine the swiftest ore shoveler, and a jackdrilling tournament to crown the strongest hammerer. On almost any day the Gold Shirt Gang might hold up the banks. Dudes pan for gold dust and nuggets and may be arrested and fined for wearing hifalutin clothing. One drink from the Hassayampa River, and they never tell the truth again. Where, but in bumpkinish Wickenburg, could the high point of the social season be the Cattle Rustler's Ball?

Mystery Valley, Midnight Mesa, Mica Mountain. Hermit's Rest, Dragoon Pass, Phantom Ranch. Rainbow Plateau, Screwtail Hill, Halfway Bend. Superstition Mountain, Devil's Kitchen, Four Corners. Agate Bridge, Apache Leap, Newspaper Rock. Whiskey Creek, Cochise Stronghold, Surprise Canyon.

Miners and prospectors impregnated their locales with measures of their loneliness and travail and recurring optimism. They christened Fools Gulch and Contention and Orphan and Poverty Knoll and the Lazy Bob. But discouraging

161

words are a bucket to the beach when compared with the Devil's Cash Box, the Old Glory, the Silverbell, the Rich-in-bar, and Gold Road. Inspiration was where the owners thought to borrow capital from a bank. A Chance was taken in Rucker Canyon in the Swisshelms. The Tip Top proved a "tip-top prospect." The Lucky Cuss derived from a brother's remark to a man who struck it rich.

Globe, grafted onto the broken ribs of the Apache Mountains of eastern Arizona, was named for a silver boulder weighing several hundred pounds and naturally etched with outlines of seven continents. The strike of silver and copper proved rich and long-lived; thus, along with the usual frame shacks, Globe acquired substantial buildings of ornate, even elegant turn-of-the-century architecture. Incongruous when new, the boxy relics are mellowed by landscaping and patina, and seem as normal as prickly pear cactus in Sixshooter Canyon and chaparral on Cousin Jack Hill.

These days in Globe, men with a few hours or many years on their hands begin gathering on the perilously steep front steps of the Gila County Courthouse. As the sun climbs, the talkers retreat upward inside a patch of shade. By midmorning they all arrive in a bunch on the second floor, where the women serve coffee and cookies for the benefit of the County Democratic Fund. The routine is older than the senior conversationalist, a facet of character of a town that exudes as much history, foot for foot, as any other in Arizona. Within three stories of hand-cut basalt are the recorded claims of the Old Dominion Mine and the vital statistics of robust men who gutted the earth and dumped the waste into drifting dunes around Globe.

On Broad Street the grandchildren of gunslingers rub shoulders with a generation twice removed from Cochise. The weddings and obituaries of the weekly newspaper no longer are segregated into Cornish, Italian, Slavic, and Mexican. Modern machines hum down the paved-over burro trails and screech where the hanging tree divided Broad near the bend in Pinal Creek.

Repelled by change, the old men of the courthouse steps retell the stories of their fathers: how, time was, San Carlos Apache women in flowing feedsack skirts, and with their babies slung in cradleboards, would window-shop for days without a penny to spend. How, back in '86, every copper penny in America was minted from Globe bullion. How, in the early days, the ore graded so high the Old Dominion could afford to import coke all the way from Wales—around the horn, and overland at $65 a ton in freight fees alone. How, lacking a railroad, Globe made it pay by packing ore to San Francisco by wagon and boat. How, one black day, three of Globe's finest miners died by fire underground, so touching the town that every worker donated a day's pay to erect the Old Dominion Memorial Library. And how, one brilliant night, Mrs. Minnie Maddern Fiske & Company arrived four hours late for performance, to find Globe Opera House still packed with Globe citizens wearing their best clothing, and how the show went on until 4 A.M. to standing ovations.

"You take the Dominion Hotel when it was new," says a snowy septuagenarian. "It had a wine cellar. Steam heat. Hot and cold baths. All the furnishings and equipment came from the East Coast. Wasn't a fancier bridal suite between Denver and San Diego."

Yes, sir. Fifty saloons and eateries that never closed. And in 1881, George W. P. Hunt with thirty cents in his pockets rode into town on a donkey, washed pots and pans in a Chinese restaurant, mucked ore for the Old Dominion, and went on to become Arizona's first state governor. Served seven terms, too. A Globe boy! And now the sun bears fully upon all the steps, and Globe's old-timers pack their memories off to shaded benches on the side streets.

Bright Angel Trail, the Maiden's Breast. Florence, Ruby, Gisela. Apache Maid Mountain. Dutch Woman Butte. Helen's Dome, Copper Queen, Sleeping Beauty Peak.

There's Growler Mountains and Swilling Gulch. What Eloy means in Arizona is a mystery, although it means "my God" in Syria. That waystop made famous in the old-time hit song, "Route 66," has a murky origin. Getting their kicks on Route 66, everybody remembers Winona, but nobody remembers the reason.

Some towns survived municipal infancy; some did not. Charmingdale lost its post office in eighteen months, but Bullhead City prospered as a playground of the Colorado River. Black Warrior was swallowed by an open-pit mine. Echo never heard a mail call. The town of Storm upped and blew away. And some towns hung on, neither very lively nor altogether dead. Walker, on Lynx Creek in the Bradshaw Mountains, is such a scatter of vague stone foundations and nests of weathered lumber. Three thousand people are gone. Their homes are collapsed, and grape and live oak camouflage eroded trails. Who were they? How did they live? What was it like to stake a claim, to find a mate, to bear a child, to found a town?

Godlike, historians probe Arizona's archives and miraculously repopulate the ghost town of Walker. Returned are the names of the first claims: The Accidental, Vinegar, Golden Fleece, Cash on Delivery. The boardinghouse serves goat's milk in its coffee. Mrs. Boblett spends a year in the wilderness without another woman to talk to, and her children pluck gold nuggets worth twenty dollars each from the creeks after heavy rains. Mrs. Milleken boils cactus

Relic Skull Valley railroad station, twenty miles southwest of Prescott, recalls a name given to the area by white travelers who found piles of bleached Indian bones, thought to be the debris of an intertribal clash.

164

into a salve which cures a cowboy's wound. George Henderson bets everybody he can freight a boiler tank to the Mud Hole Mine—and he wins with a twenty-six-horse team. One January day, Frank A. Kuhne opens his cabin door to find the snow level with his nose; and he is six feet two inches tall. Jim Breslin jumps into a mine shaft to save a boy stranded with a charge of powder and a sputtering fuse. Honest Dave Berry shoes a horse. Antonio Burrilla says, "Money nothing. One man had $80,000. Died anyway." Fred Nyberg wins the jack-drilling contest. And Thomas Barlow-Massicks, Esq., of England, is met picking fruit at Jackass Flat.

Nor is the process of name-giving finished. Peggy and Jim Kater settled in 1949 at the junction of Arizona highways 85 and 86. At first their desert homestead had no water, no electricity, no telephone. The nearest to a name was "The Y," referring to the road forking out to Ajo on the west, Tucson to the east, and Mexico to the south. Slowly the conveniences of the twentieth century arrived at the junction, along with retired folks in mobile homes and sportsmen towing boats to the Gulf of Mexico. The Katers founded a general store which ultimately attracted a post office.

When the postmaster general requested a town name, Mrs. Kater submitted "Why," along with the logical explanation, "Why do we stay in Why? We love the beautiful sunsets, the clear smog-free air, the giant cactus, the first cool breeze from the gulf on a hot summer's night, and most of all our good neighbors and friends. Why name it Why? Why not!"

With more than 30,000 students, if it were a city, Arizona State University would rank among Arizona's ten largest communities. Facilities range from 50,000-seat Sun Devil Stadium, in a saddle between two buttes, and Frank Lloyd Wright-designed Grady Gammage Auditorium, center. From the year of its founding in Tempe in 1886, ASU has been noted for its responsiveness to community needs. One example: Had ASU's engineering department not kept pace with electronics, some of the state's largest employers in manufacturing would have located elsewhere.

166

CHAPTER TEN

Cities of the Sun

One day toward the end of the 1960s when Phoenix was preparing for its centennial, a friend and I chose to lunch atop a Central Avenue tower. In unusual clarity of air, visibility extended from the Superstitions to the Estrellas, and far past Camelback to the McDowells. Every plot of ground in the 3,000-square-mile circle seemed to be serving some need or whim of man: homes and stores, parks and streets, farms and factories, inns and offices.

"Imagine if you can," said I, "that by some airborne time machine you might be suspended above this spot a century back into the past."

My guest, a Hollander, nodded.

"You could detect utterly no sign of man from here."

The Dutchman insisted, "Surely there was *something* back then."

"No. The nearest railroad was a thousand miles away. There were paddle-wheel steamers on the lower Colorado River, a week's horseback ride from here. Tucson far to the south had at most 5,000 residents, more than the rest of Arizona combined. In this stretch of the Salt River the census taker found only twenty-one families, and not one inhabitant on the original Phoenix townsite."

From 32 students in 1891, the University of Arizona has matured to an enrollment of some 30,000, representing all states and 70 foreign countries. "Lamp of the Desert," the university supports Arizona's only medical school. The University of Arizona Press is a highly regarded publisher of regional literature.

Through ranks of high-rises runs Arizona's most important road—Central Avenue of Phoenix, whose metropolitan population of a million is projected to 1,300,000 by 1980, and 2,700,000 by year 2000. Fearful of mindless growth, leaders are emerging to insist that Phoenix preserve its sense of uniqueness and quality of life.

Adding their own gifts of industry and grace to modern Arizona are substantial numbers of citizens of Oriental extraction whose enterprises include multiacre commercial flower gardens on Phoenix' southside.

Guarded by its ranks of piny ridges, Tucson has grown from a walled pueblo to a city of a third of a million inhabitants. Influenced by its Spanish origins and Mexico lying but sixty miles to the south, Tucson keeps fresh its bilingual, bicultural heritage. Cinco de Mayo, *a day of Mexican independence celebration, occasions fiestas in Tucson to rival the Fourth of July.*

Dismantled, shipped, and reconstructed stone by stone, the London Bridge incredibly has traveled from the Thames to the Colorado River, to form the nucleus of a tourist-retiree-sportsman complex at Lake Havasu City, on Arizona's western border. Projections are for five million visitors per year.

Adjacent to the pioneering retirement village of Youngton, Sun City grows in pre-planned order: lakes, open space, curved streets separating pastel homes of 17,000 senior citizens from all states of the nation.

Verbena Wrightii.

Pride of Mesa is the Arizona Mormon Temple, said to be copied after the Temple of Solomon, and open for special rites only to members of the Church of Jesus Christ of Latter-day Saints. The arboretumlike grounds are open to the public.

Tucson's brag is that every golfer there plays in the mid-70s—temperature, that is. Skyline Country Club is one of thirteen emerald-green courses with cactus-filled roughs, in the Tucson vicinity.

"Nothing?"

"From this viewpoint you would not see a road or a house or a cultivated field. Nothing."

My companion gazed again at the works of man filling the valley as far as he could see. He shook his head.

He does not believe me, I thought. He is from Amsterdam, a city that dates back to A.D. 1200. He sits in a leather chair enjoying sumptuous beef and noble burgundy in a poshly decorated, air-conditioned restaurant perched on twenty stories of beehive offices in the center of the twelfth largest (in area) and twentieth largest (in population) city of the nation. The waitress is gorgeous and graceful. Conferring at the next table are three millionaires younger than thirty-five. At the bar is a man newly arrived from Israel talking with another man who tonight will fly to Micronesia. And I am asking my guest somehow to comprehend how uncouth and uncomfortable, how violent and vacant, how gut-raw and Godawful this valley was, just a fingersnap ago, as he measures time.

Yet it is so. The white population of fledgling Phoenix in 1867 was exactly two people—a man named Smith mowing wild hay for army horses, and a drifter named Swilling, a hard-drinking entrepreneur with a plan for reopening prehistoric irrigation canals. Historian John Myers Myers states flatly, "No city in the history of the world has moved from scratch, to the attainment of such major urban standing, within the like period of time." We, who have lived through the span of greatest change, can scarcely believe it ourselves. Despite his dwelling in the eye of civilization's storm, territorial pioneer Roscoe Willson says of today's Phoenix, "To those of us who recall its horse-and-buggy days, its dusty, unpaved streets, and the leisurely air of its inhabitants, the present city seems like an Arabian Nights' dream, or one created by the touch of Aladdin's lamp."

Fair numbers of Arizonans remember the day of statehood in Phoenix, and what the town was like. The population was 22,000, and the last class to graduate from the one high school consisted of 31 boys and 17 girls. A town ditch ran along Van Buren Street. Rooms at the Commercial Hotel were $1.00 and up. M. Goldwater & Brother at First Street near Washington boasted of being "The Dry Goods Emporium of Arizona." A block away the Arizona Ostrich Farm retailed "plumes, boas, stoles, fans, tips, and novelties." Telephone number of the Cold Storage Market was Main 6. The Baswitz Cigar Company claimed, "There is no pool room in Phoenix more popular than this parlor."

Undisputed leader in campus beauty, Northern Arizona University, at Flagstaff, houses most of its students on its grounds and is closely allied with the town. University strengths are in mineral and forest sciences, education, business administration, and liberal and applied arts.

170

The smartest banker in town forecast that Phoenix would level out in growth when all agricultural lands were brought under irrigation. Eventually, one family per twenty acres would occupy the Salt River Valley, and "by the year 2000, Phoenix could well become a city of 100,000 people."

On Valentine's Day, 1912, Phoenix awaited the flash from Washington. The Westerners were snappishly aroused by federal abuse and neglect. They had endured natural disasters, scourges, and financial panic. They had fought off a Congressional threat to name them, "Gadsonia." They had heard a *laissez-faire* mining magnate cynically sneer, "Men are cheaper than timbers." They had waited overlong for water, for capital, for transportation. They had resisted joint statehood with New Mexico, and they had gambled the whole game by adopting the country's most progressive constitution.

So this was a moment of a thousand victories. At 10:03 A.M. a telegraph key stuttered the official message from President Taft, "I have this morning signed the proclamation declaring Arizona to be a state. . . ."

A stack of forty-eight sticks of dynamite voiced the people's approval in Bisbee. In Globe, a cannon spoke forty-eight times. Engineers yanked whistle cords on locomotives and mill boilers. Whiskey Row in Prescott raised a toast of "panther blood" and a hail of pistol fire. In Flagstaff, a newsman wrote, "Now, b'gosh, even the grub tastes better."

Governor-elect George W. P. Hunt received the telegram in his headquarters in the Ford Hotel. Hunt was a picture-politician of his day. Portly, bullet-headed, owlish behind circular spectacles, magnificently mustachioed, he held an occult magnetism for the masses. As a Democrat, he never let them forget that as a boy he had ridden into Arizona on a mule, and that as a man he stood aloof of the big mining companies. ("I shall never wear a copper collar.")

On Second Avenue, against Hunt's wishes, an impressive parade was forming for the march to the state capitol. Idling at the curb were gleaming horseless carriages of rich families. Hunt turned down a dozen offers to ride.

"I shall walk," he announced, lifting his voice toward the pressing crowds that would elect him six more terms. "My walk, may it be symbolic of the economies of my administration."

He ambled west on Washington. The sun wilted his carnation. He perspired and tugged at his tie and collar. He often waved his fuzzy fedora. The parade was obliged to match Hunt's snailish pace. Bands from the Indian School and the Territorial Normal School double-timed while Hunt skirted chuckholes beyond the street paving and heaved his bulk over muddy ditches. In forty-three minutes he finished the fifteen blocks. He climbed the steps to the second floor

Watery exclamation point against the dry desert sky is the world's highest fountain—560 feet—at the site of Fountain Hills, a totally planned city taking shape on nineteen square miles northeast of Phoenix. When completed, Fountain Hills is expected to be home for 70,000 residents.

of the somber stone pile often called the homeliest building in America and took the oath of office.

"My administration," he assured a crowd of 15,000, "insofar as my conduct can insure it, will be progressive. So will it be democratic, not in the narrow partisan sense the use of the word too frequently implies, but in the Jeffersonian sense denoting equality, simplicity, unostentatiousness, and economy."

A reception was followed by street dancing, star pinning, and a two-hour oration by William Jennings Bryan. It would be one of the few occasions for statewide celebration in a long, long time.

Modest predictions for Arizona held true for the next thirty years, through wars too distant to stimulate local economic growth, through depressions too crushing for a community stuck out in the middle of a desert to do much about. It was still a cow town of 65,000 residents when I first saw it in the early 1940s, when an older friend invited me along to attend a premier Phoenix attraction: the wrestling matches.

We rattled in off the Pima reservation in a tired old Chevy with a water bag flapping over a fender, up through one-drugstore towns of Chandler and Mesa and Tempe, between patches of dusty cotton where Okies and Arkies camped around their clunker cars. We moved out across the eight or nine miles of sparsely settled rolling cactusland on the north bank of the Salt River, down by the malodorous cattle pens, and on toward Phoenix. When about thirty blocks from downtown, we passed biplanes and a squadron of military trainers tied down around a squat terminal about the size of a small house. Children swam in the yellow irrigation canals. At about Sixteenth Street we encountered the first of a straggle of secondhand stores.

Waiting for fight time, we knocked around town. The streets swarmed with Saturday shoppers who had *walked* from suburbs to downtown. Posters in windows touted the sports event of the year, a girl's softball game. Indian

172

Curiosity draws a tender finger toward a barb of a golden barrel cactus in the Desert Botanical Gardens in Phoenix's Papago Park.

women in long dresses sat on the sidewalks and offered nine-petal, two-foot-wide baskets for sale for twenty dollars. "Twenty dollars?" "Well," said my older pal, "those things take three, four months to make!"

Streetcar tracks bisected main streets. Homemade candy filled the glass cases at Donofrio's. My buddy tried on a new suit at the Boston Store, but instead bought two pairs of Levi's at Porter's. We peered into the lobby of the Adams Hotel, and my mentor explained that the cattlemen talking so intently were exchanging herds of cattle on handshake agreements as binding as written contracts. We blew in twenty cents at the Penny Arcade and wandered around the city's transportation hub, the railroad station. If we had more time, my friend said, we could go out to the Carnation plant and eat some ice cream. But instead, we took seats at the counter of the American Kitchen, the city's best restaurant, and had the chef's special: breaded veal cutlet. And then we drove the seven blocks to Madison Square Garden and delivered ourselves into the yeasty, sweltering, pressurized firetrap where the Masked Marvel so repeatedly and flagrantly fouled the favorite, Red Berry, that by the second fall the good citizens of Phoenix were hurling profanity and seat cushions at the myopic referee, a full-scale riot being averted only by Red's tossing of the Marvel into the third row.

It was maybe 10 P.M. when we headed back to the reservation, encountering no more than a dozen cars as we rolled across town, by the dimmed stores, and out Washington Street where the worn-out wringer washing machines were hauled back inside locked fences of the swap stores.

"What'd you think of Phoenix?" my friend asked me.

"Is there any more to it?"

"That was it. You saw just about all there is to it."

In the decade following World War II, the lines on Arizona's economic charts tilted sharply upward, and some of the cities took on size. Young ex-servicemen, introduced to the Southwest during military training, drifted back

174

Melding with its setting of stone and scrub, the late Frank Lloyd Wright's Taliesin West is home of a foundation and fellowship which perpetuates the principals of life and form of the great architect.

to the Land of the Second Chance. Other migrants recoiled from disappointment in California. Still others were attracted by climate and opportunity and wide-open spaces. "The cowards stayed home and the weak died on the way," was the flaunt of the old days, and some of that braggadocio beat in the bosom of the plumber's helper in Dubuque who packed all his belongings in a rented trailer and informed his mother-in-law he was taking his wife and kids two thousand miles to Phoenix and look for work. In the process he became a larger person, an aware participant in the greatest movement of mankind, the twentieth-century rush to the American West. He began afresh in a city populated largely by tolerant strugglers like himself, in a state where by custom it's impolite to pry. "One hundred and ten degrees is sorta hot," he wrote home to Iowa, "but at least you don't have to shovel it off your driveway." And that made his mother-in-law wonder if *she* shouldn't look westward for a spot to retire.

In fact, certain of Arizona's chronic beginning drawbacks proved easily relieved by mid-century technology. Refrigeration made the summers bearable. Air transportation tugged Arizona into the mainstream. Revolutionary changes in communications, finance, leisure time, mobility, and lifestyles found ready acceptance in restless, plastic Phoenix, where culture was invented day-to-day, where High Society consisted mainly of coatless doers, and where if anybody kept a Blue Book it had better be in a loose-leaf binder.

By 1955 Phoenix still was small: 155,000 people in 29 square miles. For a Sunday feature, the state's leading newspaper drew up a panel of twenty conspicuous citizens to mull over the question: "What will Phoenix and Arizona be like in 1975?" Holding credentials of wisdom and vision were a mayor, a U. S. Senator, a labor union secretary, an educator, a meteorologist, a utilities executive, a minister, an anthropologist, an engineer, a banker. Their concensus:

By 1975, Phoenix would have a population of half a million, Maricopa County a million, and the state two million.

Manufacturing by far would become the state's major source of income. Tourism would come to rival agricultural production. With discovery and production of huge, low-grade deposits, mining income would double and redouble.

With legal rights to Colorado River water confirmed in court, the state would be well along with a scheme to bring that water hundreds of miles by aqueduct to central and southern Arizona. When demand exceeded the output of hydroelectric plants, the state would be turning to fossil and nuclear fuel for power production. The unconnected towns of spacious Arizona would meld into one interactive community; the character of the people would abruptly shift from decidedly rural to decidedly urban. And along with the growth, "The smog of industry. The rush of masses. The gangs of the city. Our scenic beauty commercialized . . . nature guarded by man-made walls . . . superhighways imposed on no longer remote recesses of our mountains . . . new communities surrounding new industries. With the increase in population will come enormous challenges in education, government, commerce. If we think we have a juvenile delinquency problem now, we are in for a terrible shock."

In all, it was a remarkable exercise in crystal-ball gazing, although rather conservative as things turned out. The population projections for 1975 were attained several years early. Manufacturing at about $2 billion annually indeed overtook the combined production of mining and agriculture. Between the censuses of 1950 and 1960 the population shifted dramatically from rural to urban. Tourism became a major industry. The forecasts for roads, water, and power came to pass. In lock step with progress, arrived problems.

The statistics of Phoenix, instant city, are unprecedented. In the time it took a newborn babe of the fifties to reach adulthood, a dozen high-rise buildings leaped up along Central, and more are going up, as high as forty stories. Shopping centers larger than downtown in its heyday ring a center city revitalized by a sparkling new convention center of molded concrete and venetian glass covering six blocks. Incredibly, with nine airlines and eleven transcontinental truckers and five hundred supply and warehouse firms, Phoenix has become distribution center for half the West and much of northern Mexico. Firms once hesitated to open branch offices in Phoenix; now an impressive number have moved corporate headquarters there. Building permits are issued in the tens of thousands per year. Skyscrapers are substantially leased before they are completed. It's not unusual for *thirty thousand* new households to be established in metropolitan Phoenix during a year.

By and large, Arizona's twenty-three hundred factories are non-polluters: makers of aerospace hardware and electronic components and consumer items. The state that so recently imported simple hand tools, now exports Arizona-made turbines, computers, tennis balls, air conditioners, newsprint, chain saws, apparel, telephone cable, musical instruments, and water wings for space capsules. Asked why he located in Arizona, a corporation president invariably responds: "The record of worker efficiency, low-rate of absenteeism, rock-bottom building costs, favorable business atmosphere, and of course, you can't beat the climate."

Fluttering among the stark statistics are demographic butterflies not yet netted and catalogued—Des Moines-Corpus Christi-Santa Monica mutations to confound the urbanologists. Newcomers are known to be younger, better

The first living history museum west of the Rockies, Pioneer, Arizona follows the pattern of internationally famous predecessors such as Colonial Williamsburg, Mystic Seaport, Connecticut and Sturbridge Village, Massachusetts. Pioneer, Arizona boasts of innovations . . . nature trails through nearby hills, and a campground for young travelers.

educated, higher-income achievers (inclined toward professional, technical, and service skills) than long-time residents. Of every hundred in-migrants, fourteen are from California ("lemmings in retreat"), nine from Illinois, six from Ohio, six from New York, five from Texas, five from Michigan, the rest, from elsewhere. The lure of Arizona to Midwesterners is phenomenal. In studying the feasibility of a move to Phoenix, a Milwaukee printery surveyed its four hundred employees. *All four hundred* volunteered to transfer West.

Median age of Arizonans is 24.7 years, three years below the national median. The median for Phoenix is even lower. Despite its role as a retirement town, only 7 per cent of the population is sixty-five or older. More than 40 per cent is younger than eighteen. Under the circumstances, an artificial surf could be built on a dry desert flat and become a business success. The per capita ownership of pleasure boats in oasis Phoenix equals that of San Diego, seaport. And what do the young yachtsmen of Phoenix do with their thirty thousand boats? They run them up and down the highways, in search of water. Today's hyperactive Arizonans, along with Californians, are the most mobile people on earth, with one car or light truck for every two residents. The painful provincialism of an older day has vanished—a symphony of merit performs in an elegant new concert hall; masters hang in the Phoenix Art Museum; scholars convene at the Heard Museum (of anthropology); theaters thrive on contemporary, musical, and Shakespearean stages; Van Cliburn plays in Grady Gammage Auditorium, last creation of Frank Lloyd Wright.

The Phoenix experience is repeated throughout the state. "Keep Tucson small," was a motto once proposed by the distinguished humanist Dr. Joseph Wood Krutch to the Tucson Chamber of Commerce. He might have saved his breath. If that upstart, awkward *nouveau riche* sodbuster town of Phoenix could convert its decayed downtown, could the *Old Pueblo*, with aristocratic ties to Spain and Mexico, do less? Thus, a community center with a music hall, arena, little theater, and historic restoration. If Phoenix ("Palm Beach, Red Gap, and Zenith all rolled into one") could cause spires to grow, could sophisticated Tucson not also? Thus, the metal-and-glass towers rise up out of the adobe trod by the conquistadors. And "Tucson small" exceeds a third of a million.

Until recently a two-town state, Arizona now has eight cities of populations greater than 25,000 within incorporated limits.

In 1946 when Lloyd Kiva set up Scottsdale's first crafts shop, his address was a dusty lane in a horse pasture. Into the 1950s the nickname was "Stopsdale" for its most prominent traffic control, a stop sign. Leather reins polished the hitching post outside the Pink Pony. Scottsdale's growing pains made it the butt of low humor—"Town's expanding so fast, every time they

Long a champion of native arts, Heard Museum in Phoenix regularly provides space and encouragement of Indian men and women to demonstrate their ageless skills.

From scratch in little more than a decade, the Phoenix Zoo has grown to a major and innovative displayer of animals from throughout the world.

have a fire, they have to rent a fire truck from Hertz." It's no joke now. Bedroom and bowery to neighboring Phoenix, Scottsdale has 70,000 citizens, and 8,000 swimming pools, and thirty art galleries in between thirty notable restaurants. Kiva's little leather shop multiplied into scores of blocks of specialty stores. Between 1965 and 1970 Scottsdale's population increased 566 per cent.

Rapid development also made mid-size cities of Tempe, Mesa, Glendale, Flagstaff, and Yuma; each now rivaling the Phoenix of a generation ago.

Tempe, it's economy soundly based on education, garden-type manufacturing, and service industries, seemingly sprang up like a family of mushrooms from its Grecian vale. Where so recently the showcase was a flour mill across from its landmark, a public swimming pool, Tempe as if overnight has 125 factories (most electronics-space oriented) and $2-million Big Surf, where waves large enough for surfing are mechanically produced. Aside from sprawling Arizona State University, Tempe's educational complex includes Cook Christian Training School, only one of its kind in the nation, where students from 65 Indian tribes from all parts of the nation have studied. Just yesterday, Tempe dozed amid grids of alfalfa and grain and cotton. And after a recent tour through new subdivisions, past a lake with five miles of shore, and blocks of boutiques, a veteran Arizona real estate columnist wrote, "Just where is all this going to halt?"

To Tempe's east lies Mesa, another booming community of the Salt River Valley. More so than others, Mesa was ready for the automobile, with streets laid out wide enough for Mormon founders to turn their wagons. Also a center for light industry, Mesa busies itself in agricultural operations, including food packing and processing, tourism, and activities catering to several large developments exclusively for senior citizens.

Glendale, with its own subcluster of growing towns, borders Phoenix on the west. Much of the Valley's truck garden crop, citrus and melons, grain and fiber, hay and livestock, pass through the processing plants of the west side, and in some ways, Glendale's expansion is the most startling of any in Arizona.

In 1967 Glendale issued building permits totaling $3.5 million; in 1972, the total rose to $60 million.

Opposites in climate and appearance, Flagstaff and Yuma share growth patterns tied to agriculture, tourism, and education. In alpine setting, Flagstaff still relies on its forest-products industry, but of increasing importance are its roles as gateway to northland tourism and as cultural mecca and scientific center for the northern third of Arizona. Flagstaff's Lowell Observatory and Museum of Northern Arizona probe the frontiers of diverse disciplines: astronomy and anthropology. Yuma's progress has been in big-time agriculture—where tractors may till furrows a quarter-mile long, and where groves of grapefruit and oranges may number in the tens of thousands of trees. And along with most cities of size in Arizona, Yuma has had a big-league baseball team, at least during the Cinderella days of spring training.

Alas, those forecasters of 1955, so perceptive of material progress, were also correct about concurrent human and environment dilemmas. Phoenix and its Valley have been called "not a concentration of co-operative governments, but rather a loose alliance of independent fiefdoms," or "a bunch of suburbs in search of a city." Along with its genius for growth, Phoenix has found no easy answers for traffic jams, air pollution, flood control, zoning madness, persistent slums, city planning, and second-class citizenship for many among minority races. In his presidency of the Valley Forward Association, long-time Phoenix civic leader James E. Patrick labeled Phoenix "the victim of a 'growth syndrome,' a complex ailment under any circumstances. We have been almost totally preoccupied with sheer numbers—more people, more dollars, more houses, and so on. Numbers have become the symbols of our 'success,' as well as the outward evidence of our good health. But as we have been totally preoccupied with growth, we have shown an equally strong disregard for the quality of that growth." Among proposals of Valley Forward, a broadly based committee of proven leaders, is the Rio Salado Project for transforming the eyesore of the waterless Salt River bottom into a combination flood control-aquatic park, some 20,000 reclaimed acres extending about thirty miles. The plan languishes, while a new generation of forecasters look to the year 2000, to a Phoenix of three million, to an airport with seven times as many customers, to three times as many automobiles, to the fifth largest megalopolis in the nation.

Neil Morgan, analyst of the West and disinterested critic of Phoenix, has written in his *Westward Tilt,* "Phoenix is in its golden era because everyone is a pioneer. What Arizona lacks in social consciousness is compensated for just now by abundance. But some year soon, unless it can resist the American pattern, power factions will begin to divide the city; banking interests or busi-

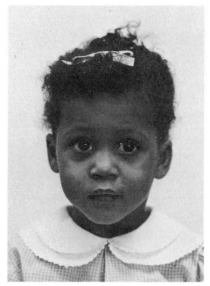

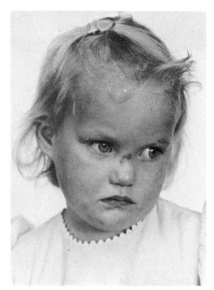
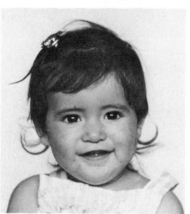
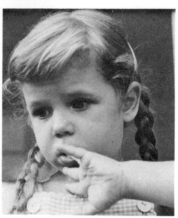

The future of Arizona

ness combines and labor unions will carve out niches of control for more selfish gain; and spontaneity, initiative, and enterprise will begin to fade. There is hope, however, that Phoenix will resist the trend . . . that it will hold tight to its economic and political independence."

The oft-heard prayer in Arizona is, "Please, not another Los Angeles." Yet that is precisely the prospect, in the opinion of futurist Robert Theobald, himself an Arizona resident. He says Arizona can be the last of the old states, or the first of the new, that "Arizona, the West, Midwest, and South have some very real opportunities to change the country." Above all, says Theobald, Arizona has to have a dream, "has to decide that it has something that is valuable, inherent in itself. It has to develop a purpose for itself which is related to its past and its possible future, and believe in itself."

The alternative was symbolically (and not altogether innocently) described by the philosopher Dick Wick Hall in an issue of the *Salome Sun* in 1923: "All right, if you are in such a Hurry to get to Los Angeles. Head Lizzie right down the road beside the railroad Track and turn sharp to the Left where the Depot used to be before they Moved it away; four miles more and you come to the Windmill at Desert Well and the New Road across the Dry Lakes and keep right on going; 30 miles from Salome you pass the forks of the road leading to the Apache Mine. Go and see it or keep right on to Quartzsite, 39 miles from Salome, where you can get anything you want; 19 miles past Quartzsite you come to the Ferry across the Colorado River and five miles the other side of the River is Blythe, the Metropolis of the rich Palo Verde farming country . . . 45 miles from Blythe you come to Desert Center and 45 miles more brings you to Mecca, where the Paved Road starts to Los Angeles. If you have gotten this far and can't follow a paved road on into Los Angeles, then there's no use in my trying to tell you what to do."

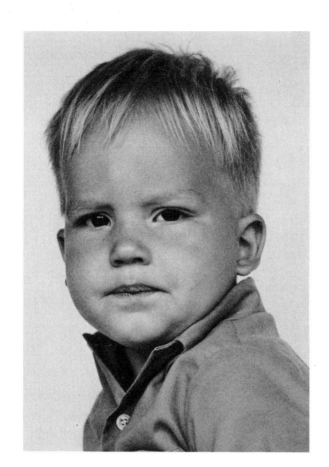

INDEX

Note: photos are indicated by *italicized* numbers

190

This book is set in the phototype
version of Herman Zapf's Palatino.
Typographic design and calligraphy
by Joseph P. Ascherl